EDUCATION IN INDIA

EDUCATION IN INDIA

WILLIAM I. CHAMBERLAIN, M.A.

GYAN

Published by

Gyan Publishing House
5, Ansari Road
Daryaganj, New Delhi-110002
Phone: 011-47034999, 9811692060
E-mail: books@gyanbooks.com

Distribution Network
gyanbooks.com
India, USA, Canada, UK, Australia, France

ISBN : 978-81-212-9520-8 (PB)
First Published, 1899

2nd Impression 2023

Printed at: Gyan Press, Delhi.

EDUCATION IN INDIA
Author: WILLIAM I. CHAMBERLAIN

EDUCATION IN INDIA

BY

WILLIAM I. CHAMBERLAIN, M. A.

SUBMITTED IN PARTIAL FULFILLMENT OF THE REQUIREMENTS
FOR THE DEGREE OF DOCTOR OF PHILOSOPHY
IN THE
FACULTY OF PHILOSOPHY
COLUMBIA UNIVERSITY

1899

CONTENTS

PART I

INTRODUCTORY

CHAPTER I

CHAPTER II

PART II

EDUCATION UNDER BRITISH RULE

CHAPTER I

CHAPTER II

HISTORY (*Continued*). PAGE

Second Period, 1823–1854.

CHAPTER III

HISTORY (*Continued*).

Third Period, 1854–1882.

CHAPTER IV

PAGE

HISTORY (*Concluded*).

Fourth Period, 1882–1898.

CHAPTER V

B. PRESENT CONDITION OF EDUCATION IN INDIA.

CHAPTER VI

C. PROBLEMS OF NATIONAL DEVELOPMENT.

EDUCATION IN INDIA

PART I

INTRODUCTORY

CHAPTER I

It might, perhaps, be thought natural to introduce the treatment of the subject of this paper with a consideration of the country, the civilization, and the religions of the Hindus, all of which are so closely allied to a study of education in India. But the necessity for such preliminary discussion is not so apparent when we remember the availability, at the present day, of information with regard to the life and the civilization of people inhabiting the most distant portions of the earth, the large place which the English language and literature are now occupying in the changing civilization of the Orient, and the predominance of Eastern questions in the rapidly developing history of our time, so largely recorded in our own language.

Civilization and Moral Conceptions. It is quite impossible, however, to give anything approaching to a correct view of what constitutes the education of a people, without first putting before us an outline, at least, of that people's civilization; and civilization resolves itself, for educational purposes, into the religious and moral conceptions of a nation, and its consequent social and political organizations.

To treat of the characteristics of a nation's life in detail is quite foreign to our purpose, and would tend to obscure the precise object of the educational historian. What chiefly concerns us, as students of the education of a people without specific educational institutions, is to bring into view the religious idea, as the ultimate expression of the national life, avoiding, at the same time, the temptation to linger over the country and people.

The Religious Ideals, Clue to Educational System. What is true of the development of the German school system, in more recent times, is also true of the developing of the educational system of India in past centuries: the clue must be found in the religious ideals, as tempered by prevailing social and political influences. Indeed, it has always been true that the presence of a dominant force in the life of a nation is seen to bring about some change in the educational system, making for the permanence of the existing ideals, or their expulsion, according to the aims of the leaders of the movement. And never have forces been found so dominant, or so calculated to take a deep hold upon the life of a people, as these conditioned religious ideals.

This preliminary recognition of the religious element among a given people must, of necessity, be followed by a fuller statement of the means which the State has, more or less consciously, adopted to bring up its children with a view to maintaining its ideals and its national life, in so far as its records make this possible.

Civilization of India. The earliest civilization of India may be embraced within 2000 to 1400 B. C., the period of tradition and of primitive Aryan survivals.

Whitney says that all dates set up in Indian literary history are pins set up to be bowled down again.[1] A liberal margin of possible error must be allowed in the assumption of any specific dates. For none of the Indian religious

[1] Whitney, *A Sanskrit Grammar*. Introduction, p. 19.

works have we a certain date. Nor is there for any one of the earlier compositions the certainty that it belongs, as a whole, to any one time. They are the gleanings of the centuries. The general compass of the enormous literature of India is from an indefinite antiquity to about 1500 A. D. The weight of scholarship seems to be in favor of provisionally assuming 2000 B. C. as the starting point of Hindu literature.[1]

Writings. The writings which embody the intellectual and moral faiths of the Hindus are:

A. The Vedas, consisting of prayers and praise and ritualistic precepts, dating perhaps about 1200 B. C., although there is good authority for a much earlier date.

B. The Upanishads, or the secret doctrine, written in prose, and largely of the nature of commentaries on the Vedas.

C. The Code of Manu, a collection of traditionary usages and customs, of a social, domestic, and political character, and abounding in excellent moral precepts, dating from about 300 B. C. to 100 B. C.[2]

In addition to these, we find a Literature, in the modern sense. The tales of heroes, which were, originally, traditional, reached a literary form in the great epics, which have reference to an early state of society; but they took their present form in, perhaps, 300 B. C. and 100 B. C.[3]

These are:

D. The Ramayana, which presents, in a continuous story, a high type of human life.

E. The Mahabharata, which has been called an encyclopedia of tradition.

[1] Hopkins, *Religions of India*. Introduction, p. 3. Shroeder, *Indiens Litera tur und Cultur*.

[2] Lanman, *A Sanskrit Reader*. Notes, p. 345.

[3] Hopkins, *Indian Literature in World's Best Literature*.

These epics are the highest literary expression of the Hindu mind, and have exercised a great influence on the life of the people of India.

Apart from these more formal writings, embodying the intellectual and moral faith of the Hindus, there are later and simpler collections of traditionary, oral, village teaching, containing fables, allegories, and parables. These fireside tales were numerous, and they very largely influenced the faith of the simpler folk. The oldest of these collections of popular stories is

The Panchatantra. It dates from about the Vth century A. D., and was translated in the VIth into the Persian and Arabic, thence into several of the languages of Asia, and later into a number of the languages of Europe.

Governing Idea. Through the whole system of Vedic thought there runs one general, governing idea, the omnipenetrativeness of the Deity, as it has been called, or a spiritual pantheism. The practical effects of this pantheistic temperament were conspicuous in the fact that the highest aim of the Hindu is abnegation of life, with a view to the absorption of the individual into the "All." Transmigration was only a step in the process of absorption. Before the All-One, the individual is of no moment. Such an idea, if rooted in the nature of a people, is an effective check to all self-reliant activity, weakens all sense of individual responsibility, and destroys the ambition of excellence. Ascetic contemplation becomes the supreme virtue in religion. Thus the ethical virtues of a people whose deepest convictions are pantheistic, and whose highest hopes are of personal absorption in the universal, are such as temperance, patience, docility, gentleness and resignation. These are naturally accompanied by politeness, respect for parents and elders, and obedience to the powers that be, both civic and ecclesiastic.

But duty, in the old Greek sense, or in our commanding sense of the word, and the virtues flowing from a strong personality which controls circumstances, and shapes the life, were not to be expected, nor were they found.

The aim of Education. The end of education is thus expressed in Manu's Book of Laws:

"Studying the Veda, (practising) austerities, (the acquisition of true) knowledge, the subjugation of the organs, abstention from doing injury, and serving the Guru [the spiritual teacher] are the best means for attaining supreme bliss."[1]

The educational significance of this religious and ethical system lay in the fact that it was the natural expression of the real Hindu mind, which was dreamy and metaphysical. It is, however, worthy of note that Hinduism was not, in its origin and essence, a religion of externalism. It was the inner life of the soul that was of moment, and when this was lost sight of, Buddhism arose. When sacrifice and ceremonial began to supersede the intellectual aad ethical elements of Brahmanism, the reform that Buddhism attempted, followed.

But the effect of Buddhistic teaching on the Hindu mind was not an awakening of the individuality; for, while the God of Brahmanism was a union with the absolute Being, not to be distinguished from absorption, the God of Buddhism was extinction of the individual, not to be distinguished from non-existence. In both cases individuality was gone.

Effect of Teaching. This brief summary of the Hindu philosophy of life, as influenced by both Brahmanic and Buddhistic thought, will enable us to understand the very theoretical character of ancient education in India. Wuttke strikingly contrasts it with even the neighboring Oriental, but more practical, system of ethics taught by Confucius in China:

[1] Translation of G. Bühler in *The Sacred Books of the East*, Vol. XXV., xii. 83. Compare also chapter on "Studentship," ii. 6–249.

"The Chinese," says he, "educate for practical life, the Indians for the ideal; those for earth, these for heaven; those educate their sons for entering the world, these for going out of it; those educate for citizenship, these for priesthood; those for industrial activity, these for knowledge; those teach their sons the laws of the state, these teach them the essence of the Godhead; those lead their sons into the world, these lead them out of the world into themselves; those teach their children to earn and enjoy, these to beg and to renunciate."

Caste. When we approach the subject of education in India we are met by the great, all-influencing socio-religious fact of *Caste*, a system which grew up, gradually, and which claims to be as old as the Vedas.[1] This caste system determined the character and the area of the education. While its origin may have been based upon social conditions, it came to have a religious sanction, and its observance became largely the religion of the people.

External Influences. While we must recognize the presence of a permanent influence—the Brahman Caste System—throughout the long story of the study of letters, and of the preservation of culture in India, there were other influences, external to Brahmanism, that entered into, and affected, for a time, the development of education in India. These were not, however, of a permanent character, and it cannot be said that they changed the course of the history of education among the Hindus. These external influences were Buddhism and Muhammadanism.

a. Buddhism. The Buddhistic Reformation began about 500 B. C., but it was only from about 250 B. C. that it formulated itself as a rival of Brahmanism. In 500 A. D., Brahmanism again gained the ascendency, and Buddhism was exiled to

[1] Kaeki, *Rig Veda*. Translation by Arrowsmith, p. 17 and p. 114, note 56.

Ceylon in the South, Thibet in the North, and Burmah, China and Japan in the East.

Buddhistic Education. Of Buddhistic Education[1] it may be said, in general, that the people were upon a perfect equality, as the teaching of Buddha was, in part, a protest against the divisions of caste. All were alike interested in the common routine, which was everywhere the same, embracing reading and writing in the vernaculars, and some smattering of knowledge of the sacred Pali text. These schools had no direct revenues, the priests being dependent upon the free-will offerings of the people for their subsistence. Usage imposed upon parents the duty of feeding the clergy of the colleges in which their children were being educated. A large number of scholars, therefore, formed the best endowment. These schools were attended by girls, on the same terms. With the exception of the schools in Burmah, and of a few large collegiate monasteries in Ceylon and in northern India, Buddhism, as an educational force, has long since passed out of India.

b. Muhammadanism. From about the time of the final expulsion of Buddhism from India, Muhammadanism was a controlling force in the political life of that country, for ten centuries.

Muhammadan Education. But the history of Muhammadan education in India offers few temptations for investigation. Everywhere guiltless of a system, it was more than usually fragmentary in a country where Moslem rule was so often synonymous with anarchy. There were attached to the mosques the usual classes for studying the Koran. We are told also that the Emperor, Aurungzeb, established universities in all the principal cities, and erected schools in the smaller towns, providing them with libraries and endowments. But how much of this was theory, and how much practice and actuality, must be left undecided, for evidence is wanting to establish the latter condition.

[1] Asiatic Journal, 1841, No. 34.

Character of Schools. To the Musalman, the essence of all literature and science is summed up in the Koran, and even the most ignorant of the faithful know a few verses, whether they understand the language or not. Their two sacred languages are the Persian and the Arabic. Mr. Adam found in his inquiries, which will be referred to more particularly in the succeeding chapter, that the Persian schools were chiefly elementary, while the Arabic were more advanced.

Elementary Schools. The Muhammadan elementary schools were literary and philological in character, and employed a learned language. They had, withal, a commercial value, inasmuch as throughout the Musalman rule, and under the English, until 1835, Persian was the language of the courts of law in India. To this fact was due the otherwise surprising circumstance that quite half the number of students in Persian schools were Hindus, largely of the Brahman caste.

Advanced Schools. In the advanced schools, however, the language employed was the Arabic, and the students were, to a man, Musalmans. In these schools there were complete courses in rhetoric, logic, law, ritual and theology. Euclid and Ptolemy's Astronomy were familiar in translations, and other branches of Natural Philosophy were followed. Indeed, Arabic learning was not unknown in Europe.

Although the advanced schools, few in number, attained to such heights in scholastic acquirement, and although the Musalman power was dominant in India during so many centuries, the Islamic faith was so foreign to the country, and so iconoclastic in its relations and contact with other religions of the Hindus, that Muhammadanism never became a force in the social or educational life of the people. It never was more than an external influence, although its following constitutes one-fifth of the population of India.

CHAPTER II

INDIGENOUS EDUCATION

WHILE the preponderating influence of religious ideals upon the development of education in India is a fact, as already recognized and emphasized, there is no country where the love of learning had an earlier origin, or exercised a more lasting or powerful influence, than in India. From the poets of the Vedic age to the Bengali philosopher of the present day, there has been an uninterrupted succession of teachers and scholars. The immense literature which this long period has produced is penetrated with the scholastic spirit. The ancient Hindu theory of education is contained, as already pointed out, in the comprehensive volume, the Institutes of Manu.

Learning in Earliest Times.

Vicissitudes.

During the fifteen centuries ending with the tenth of our era, learning, no doubt, experienced many vicissitudes of popularity and unpopularity. Different teachers and seats of learning probably acquired and lost great reputations, and knowledge, under monarchs of varying temperament, was doubtless alternately patronized and eclipsed in camps and cities.

Permanent Influence.

But there was one permanent influence universally present which preserved the study of letters from utter annihilation. This was the authorfty of the Brahman caste. It was to this spiritual authority that India owed the preservation of her culture through long periods of darkness which history has not yet succeeded in penetrating.

Government Inquiries.

It was not until the year 1820 that interest began to be aroused in the subject of indigenous education in India, and that English researches discovered the state of native education in operation. At that time, Government was induced to make careful inquiries, preparatory to undertaking and instituting fresh measures of its own. Of these inquiries, the three most important were conducted in the Presidencies of Madras, Bombay, and Bengal, commencing in 1822, 1823, and 1835, respectively. These were set on foot by three of the most eminent British Governors who ever ruled in India, Sir Thomas Munro, of Madras, Lord Elphinstone, of Bombay, and Lord William Bentinck, of Bengal. Later, inquiries were instituted in the other minor provinces; but a brief reference to these three important researches will suffice for our present purpose.

Sir Thomas Munro (1822), Madras.

In the year 1822, Sir Thomas Munro, Governor of Madras, ordered an investigation[1] to be made into the state of indigenous education in that Presidency. His reasons were the rapid decay of literature and the arts, and the deep ignorance in which the masses of the people were sunk. He felt it to be one of the chief duties of the East India Company to provide for the "moral and intellectual amelioration" of the condition of the people. The results of these inquiries were made known in 1826, in which year Sir Thomas reported to the Court of Directors, as follows:[2]

"It appears that the number of schools and what are called colleges in the territories under this Presidency, amount to 12,498, and the population to 12,850,941: so that there is one school to every one thousand of the population; but, as only a very few females are taught in schools, we may reckon one school to every 500 of the population." He concludes: "I am inclined to estimate the portion of

[1] Minute dated June 25, 1822.

[2] Minute dated March 10, 1826.

the whole population who receive school education to be nearer one-third than one-fourth of the whole. . . . . The state of education exhibited, low as it is, compared with that of our own country, is higher than it was in most European countries at no very distant times."

Lord Elphinstone (1823), Bombay. Lord Elphinstone's researches in Bombay were set on foot in the year 1823, from the same motives as were those of Munro. Their results were communicated in a Minute to the Council in 1832:

"It appears that, in the British territories dependent on Bombay, containing a population of 4,681,735 souls, there are 1705 schools, at which 35,143 seholars are receiving education."

According to Munro's calculation, it follows that, in the Bombay Presidency, only one in eight boys of the proper age (between 5 and 10 years) was receiving any instruction. As elsewhere in India, there was little trace of female education.

Lord Bentinck (1835), Bengal. In 1835 Lord Bentinck instituted similar inquiries, appointing Mr. Adam to investigate the state of education in Bengal. His three Reports appeared in 1835, 1836, and 1838. From the accuracy of their information, the candor, sense, and statesmanship of their author, these Reports are among the most valuable, authoritative, and interesting publications extant on education in India.

Mr. Adam's Reports. The general results arrived at by Mr. Adam for Bengal were these:

In a population of 7,789,152, there were 3,355 schools, with 41,247 scholars. In a population of 692,270 there were 2,414 children being taught at home, which, for the former population, would represent about 28,000 scholars. Of the adult male population, an average of about 5.55 per cent. could read and write. On the whole, about 7.8 per cent. of children of school age were being taught at school, and over 5.2 per cent. at home, giving a total percentage of 13.

Character of Native Schools.

The character of the schools, as determined by these researches, seemed to correspond with the period examined. At the period of transition from the Vedic to the Brahmanic stage of religious development, about 1200 B. C., the *Courts of the Kings* were the centres of culture. Priests were attached to these courts, and, in connection with them, there grew up schools for the studying and handing down of sacred hymns and sacrificial practices. At a later period, 1000 B. C., there arose Brahmanic settlements, called Parishads, which we might call *Collegiate* institutions of learning. In their beginnings, these Parishads were constituted by three able Brahmans in a village, learned in the Vedas, and competent to maintain the sacrificial fire. To these centres, men who wished to devote their lives to learning might go, and receive instruction in the Vedas.

Court Schools, 1200 B. C.

Collegiate Institutions. 1000 B. C.

Megasthenes, the Greek historian who lived in India three centuries B. C., seemed to imply the existence of schools suited to the four great divisions of caste.

Caste Schools, 300 B. C.

These were:

1. The Brahman schools, whose exclusive function was to educate Priests and Teachers.

2. The Warrior Schools, whose function was to train the pupils to martial exercises.

3. The Industrial Schools, whose method seemed to be the apprentice system; and,

4. The Lowest Schools, where the training was for, and by means of, menial work.

Of Female Education there was none.

Modern Schools.

In more modern times, the schools discovered by the Government inquiries under present reference, were of two kinds, so far as the preponderating Hindu community was concerned. Distinctively Buddhistic and Muhammadan schools, built upon the religious ideals of those comparatively small communities, have been noted in the preceding chapter.

For the education of the Hindus there were:

1. Elementary Schools, or Patasalas:

2. Schools of Learning, or Tols, corresponding to the Parishads, or ancient collegiate institutions.

Patasalas, Elementary Schools. The elementary schools existed in most of the villages of India, a country largely given up to agriculture. In the early morning, the few lads would assemble in the village shed, or under the shade of a wide-branching tree. The teachers, who were village officers, were supported by presents given on leaving at the end of the year, or period of service, or by monthly or weekly gifts in grain, food, or clothing, the whole not averaging above Rs. 5, or possibly $2.00 per mensem. Though belonging to the caste of writers, or scribes, they were little respected and poorly rewarded.

The teaching was oral, both books and manuscripts being then unknown. The boys commenced their attendance at school at about the age of five, and continued for five years, progressing through four stages. The first was occupied with learning the vowels and consonants, and tracing them with their fingers, on a sand floor. During the second period the boys were taught to write on the palm leaf, with a reed pen, connecting vowels and consonants, and they were also taught tables of numeration, weight, measure, and money. In the third period, they studied the rules of arithmetic and the elements of mensuration. The last period was devoted to advanced arithmetic, to accounts, and to the composition of letters written on paper. The orthography of the native languages was not required in the Patasalas. These schools were resorted to chiefly by the sons of the merchant and banking classes. The amount of learning imparted was largely dependent upon the diligence and capacity of the masters. On the whole, the teachers seem to have been fairly conscientious, regarding their occupation as one with a long and honorable tradition.

Schools of Learning. Tols. The Schools of Learning were entirely unconnected with the Patasalas, or Village Schools. So complete was the severance that the preliminary instruction necessary for entrance to the Tols was generally obtained, not in the Patasalas, but at home. Although only in the proportion of one to three in the number of schools, and one to ten in the number of scholars, the Tols bore a higher reputation than the Patasalas. While, theoretically, the study of grammar, rhetoric, poetry and astronomy was open to the inferior castes, all higher education, except medicine, was imparted only by Brahman teachers and received only by Brahman boys. Mr. Adam writes, in his reports, in the highest terms of the teachers in these schools. Although living amid the humblest surroundings, unpretentious and simple in their manner, these men were adepts in the subtleties of the profoundest grammar of what is probably the most philosophical language in Asia, if not in the world, the Sanskrit. They were skilled in the niceties of its usage, and in the principles of its structure. They were familiar with their national laws and literature, and indulged in the most abstruse disquisitions in logic and ethical philosophy. They were the visible representatives of culture and religion, and of all the higher forces in the Hindus.

These schools were not supported by fees, which are forbidden by the Institutes of Manu. At the end of the course, the scholars made a present to their Master. Not infrequently the school possessed a small endowment of land. Bound together by common study of sacred books, and by close ties of caste, the intercourse between teacher and scholar resembled that which Fichte conceived.

The course of study lasted for as much as 20 years, from the 10th to the 30th year. They did not attempt to teach the whole circle of sciences. At an early date special schools sprang up, of Literature, Law, Logic, Mythology, Medicine and Vedanta. The general characteristics of instruction were impracticability and thoroughness. The pandit was indifferent to the due proportion of things, and careless of the flight of time. Commentaries on commentaries were committed to memory. Arguments laboriously built up one day were declared fallacious the next, and as laboriously refuted. This kind of training produced its characteristic results—an unworldliness, a want of practical sagacity, an intellectual isolation, and intensified class feeling, stronger than has been known in any other country. But, with these limitations and incongruities, the authority possessed by these schools and teachers through so many centuries was unquestioned, and limited only by Cape Cormorin and the Himalayas.

Summary. Such was the character and extent of the native education revealed by these early English researches. On the average, about one boy in ten of the proper age was receiving some kind of indigenous education. The lower orders were entirely uninstructed. The classes of middle rank received a scanty and strictly commercial training. On the other hand, every Brahman was able to read and write, and a considerable body of this class had partaken of what may be styled a liberal education, while not a few had, further, obtained some eminence in such studies as grammar, rhetoric, mathematics and metaphysics. In physical science their knowledge was infinitely inferior to that current in Europe at the corresponding date. In these more practical branches, real progress had ceased for centuries. But the attainments of the Hindus were not inferior to those of any ancient nation, nor, indeed, to those of Europe, prior to the Renaissance.

Moreover, these inquiries in the early part of this century found education, like all else in India, in a state of decline, due to the anarchy and oppression which had protracted the people's energies for three or four centuries, or since the crumbling away of the great Moghul Dynasties.

PART II

EDUCATION UNDER BRITISH RULE

CHAPTER I

Introduction. HAVING thus placed before ourselves the predominating religious ideals, and the consequent educational system among the people of India, we are now prepared to enter upon the consideration of the most important phase of our inquiry, and that which concerns us most from a practical standpoint, viz., Modern Education in India: its history and organization and its present condition.

We shall frequently be called upon to observe how largely this has been furthered by the pre-existence of a wide-spread system, and how large a part of the schools now in operation are hardly more than reconstructions of the ancient indigenous schools which we have found to have existed in almost every village.

The Period. The story of Modern Education in India covers, for the most part, the period of the XVIIIth and XIXth centuries, and it is European in its character, the predominating influences being Scotch and English. Although contributions were made by the Dutch, the Portuguese, the Danish, the French and the German, these have not been of a sufficient extent, nor have they covered a sufficient period of time to entitle them to be considered as separate influences affecting the development of the modern British system superimposed upon the ancient, indigenous system, so long-lived and so wide-spread in India.

Its Influence. It is only of late years that British Education has commenced to take root in the soil of India. Like other parts of that striking experiment whereby the newest European methods are being applied to the re-organization of a long stationary Asiatic Society, it has yet to adapt itself entirely to changed conditions, to minds differently constituted, and to divergent modes of thought. To the present time its history has been one of measures and statistics. And it will be long before the changes which are at work in Hinduism will result in characteristic movements in definite directions. As yet, we dare not predict with certainty what place modern British Education will finally hold in its theories, and what share the Sanskrit Literature and Brahmanic Philosophy will retain of its affection and regard.

Its Treatment. In the treatment of British Education in India, we shall deal with it under three phases:

A. Its History and Development.

B. Its Present Condition.

C. Its Chief Problems of the Present and the Future.

A. *History and Development.*

Modern, or European, education in India covering, as we have said, the last two centuries, has passed through four well-defined stages:

1. The *first* begins early in the eighteenth century, and ends in about 1823, when government inquiries were instituted into the state of indigenous education. It was a period of almost exclusively private effort, with only occasional government participation, the ulterior object of which was the conciliation of the people.

2. The *second* period ends with the great Despatch of the Court of Directors, drawn up by Sir Charles Wood, in 1854, and called the Magna Charta of English education in India. This established something like uniformity in the place of

the previously divergent administrations, and placed government participation in the education of the people upon sound principles.

3. The *third* period extends to the Education Commission of 1882–3. At this time, a careful inquiry was entered upon as to the workings of the system during the quarter century of its establisment, and changes were made looking to its better adaptation to the altered conditions and to the new developments.

4. The *fourth* period has to do with the last two decades, commencing with the appointment and labors of the Education Commission, during which strenuous efforts have been made by Government, and private bodies, to strengthen the educational system, and to include within its beneficent influence the lower castes, and the great number of the outcastes, the Panchamma, or fifth class, as falling entirely without the four great divisions of caste, and constituting one-sixth of the population.

First Period. 1706–1823. In India, as so often elsewhere, the pioneers in education were the missionaries.

Omitting the labors of Xavier, at Goa, in the sixteenth century, and of the Dutch, in Ceylon, in the seventeenth, the first teachers who enter into this period were the early Danish missionaries, Ziegenbalg, Schulze and Schwartz. Arriving in Tranquebar in 1706, the first of these set themselves at once to study the vernaculars, with a view to teaching. The schools established by this Mission at no time contained any large number of pupils. The maximum number never rose above 500. But the history of this Danish Mission is interesting, not only because of the ability and character of its missionaries, but, also, and especially, because it narrates the earliest attempts at Protestant education, which has now attained so great a development in India. It has another special interest for us, inasmuch as these Danish missionaries came in contact with

The Danish Mission.

almost all the fundamental questions which have aroused discussion in connection with education in India, and some of which are still vehemently debated. Some of these questions were:

Educational Questions.

a. The Desirability of Religious Instruction, which was affirmatively maintained by them.

b. The Choice of the Language to be employed, which was decided in favor of the Vernaculars, in the large number of schools, English only being used in seminaries and normal classes, as the most convenient means of giving access to the stores of European knowledge.

c. The Production of a Vernacular Literature, which they accomplished, in part, through the translation of the Bible, and the publication of dictionaries and school-books for their own schools.

English Missions. S. P. C. K.

In the year 1727, the first English Mission was established in India, the Society for Promoting Christian Knowledge. This Society secured the services of the great Danish missionary, Schwartz, who arrived in India in 1760, and who was their chief agent in establishing schools in a number of the large cities in Southern India. This illustrious pioneer did more than any other man in the eighteenth century for Christianity and for education in India.

Baptist Society.

The close of this century saw the appearance of the third missionary society, that of the English Baptists, whose field of labor was Bengal, and whose chief representatives were Carey, Ward, Grant and Marshman, all men of ability and distinction. They were able, by their Oriental scholarship, to provide schools of a higher grade.

Other Societies.

At the beginning of the nineteenth century, a great impnlse was given to missionary and educational enterprise. The London, the Wesleyan and the Church Missionary Societies began to plant stations and schools in Eastern and Southern India. It is probable that at the close of this first period there were about 15,000 children under tuition in these mission institutions.

Their Character and Service to Education. Elementary and precarious as was the character of most of these schools, from the very nature of the circumstances, obstructed by the prejudices of the government and the fears of the people, this early missionary education is, nevertheless, interesting as the beginning of a now widely prevalent system. Its chief importance lay, however, in the fact that it was the means of attracting the attention of the Government, both in India and in England, to what was a plain duty.

Early Government Attempts. The first project for native education which can be ascribed to Government, was a scheme propounded in 1784 for establifhing English schools for the

Madras. higher classes of every province. With the assistance of the missionary, Schwartz, a few schools were started, but they do not seem to have increased in number.

Calcutta. In the same year, also, Warren Hastings, then Governor-General, determined upon the establishment of an Arabic College in Calcutta, with the double object of arresting the decay of Oriental learning, and of encouraging good feeling between the English and their subjects.

Benares. This Muhammadan institution in Calcutta was followed, in 1791, by the Sanskrit College at Benares, the ancient sacred city of the Hindus. The real object of the founding of the latter was clear from the proposed course of study, which included the entire curriculum of Hindu study. The promotion of Orientalism was, thenceforth, until the famous minute of Macaulay, in 1835, the settled policy of Government.

Summary. Within this first period, therefore, there were in operation the three kinds of education now carried on in India, Indigenous, Missionary and Government. Henceforth, Government Education will engage most of our attention. The other two will need only occasional references.

CHAPTER II

Second Period, 1823–54.

It has often been remarked, and not without many illustrations of its truth, that most measures of reform which have benefited India since it came under British rule have been mainly advocated and effected in England. This appeal, apparently from the well-informed to the ignorant, has been in reality, in the past, an appeal from Justice in India to Justice Universal. This is illustrated in connection with educational reforms inaugurated in the period now under consideration.

Educational Reforms. The Royal Charter, under which the East India Company operated its great possessions in India, was renewable every twenty years. In 1793 the proposals of Wilberforce to introduce an educational clause into the charter failed; but in 1813, reinforced by Grant, he revived the proposal. In an essay upon the Condition of the People of India they claimed that, "by planting our language, our knowledge, our opinions, and our religion in our Asiatic territories we shall put a great work beyond the reach of contingencies. We shall, probably, have wedded the inhabitants of these territories to this country; but, at any rate, we shall have done an act of strict duty to them, and a lasting service to mankind."

Charter of 1813. Parliament came to see that, in a large view of the circumstances, it was the duty of England to improve the state of knowledge among her subjects in India, and the following regulation was included in the Charter of 1813: "That a sum of not less than one lakh (100,000) of Rupees in each year shall be set apart and applied to the founding and maintaining of colleges, schools, public lectures, and other institutions for the revival and improvement of literature, for the encouragement of the learned natives of India, and for the introduction and promotion of a knowledge of the sciences among the inhabitants of the British territories in India."

Application of Grant. The Court of Directors were not a little embarrassed as to the disposal of the Rs. 100,000 a year with which, contrary to their wish, they found themselves presented. They, however, communicated with the Governor-General in 1814, proposing to expend this grant from their own revenues, not in building new colleges, but in improving those already in existence, and in inspiring their younger civil servants with the desire to study the Sanskrit language, by the offer of liberal rewards. Notwithstanding these official proposals, it was said by Sir Charles Trevelyan, in his work on Education in India,[1] that, until 1823 no steps were taken to carry out the orders of Parliament. This statement, however, does not seem to be entirely borne out by the official report of Government expenditures on Education during the years 1813–30.

Committee of Public Instruction. At any rate, the first decisive step was the appointment of a "Committee of Public Instruction," in 1823. This Board was charged with the yearly expenditure of the lakh of rupees voted by Parliament, and all the institutions at that time maintained by the Government were placed under its authority.

Institutions. These included an English College, six Oriental Colleges, and a number of elementary schools in Bengal and Rajputana. The Committee, however, did not confine itself to this scant organization, but gave its attention, also, to
Press. the publication of Oriental books. A press was

[1] 1835.

started in 1824, and received a monthly grant of Rs. 700. Great as was the benefit that Sanskrit and Arabic scholarship in England and on the Continent received, as an educational expedient for India it was an embarrassing failure, and ceased to operate in 1835.

1823–1833. It would be useless to follow, in any detail, the Proceedings of the Committee from 1823 to 1833. During that period no new principle was enunciated, and but a very few new institutions were founded. The only innovation of any importance was the establishment of classes in English in all the chief colleges. Stipends were general, and were conferred without any regard to proficiency.

Dr. Alexander Duff. In 1830, Dr. Alexander Duff arrived in Calcutta as the Missionary of the General Assembly of the Scotch Kirk, and as the leader of the great educational work inaugurated by that mission, and carried on for so many years by that and the Free Church of Scotland Mission. Dr. Duff established a school in Calcutta, and chose the English language as the vehicle for conveying knowledge, and the science and literature of Europe as the subject. This school was an eminent success, and the Hindus flocked thither in large numbers. The excellence of the teaching, and the results of the public examinations, soon made the school favorably and widely known, and this fact gave weight to the articles which Dr. Duff contributed on the celebrated controversy which now arose, and which only closed with Macaulay's famous Minute, in 1835, on the advantages of English over Sanskrit and Arabic, as a medium of instruction.

The Charter of 1833. When the Royal Charter was renewed in 1833, Parliament increased the funds placed at the disposal of the Committee from Rs. 100,000 to Rs. 1,000,000.

Enhanced Grant. The question as to the employment of this enhanced sum aroused one of the most violent controversies which have ever taken place in the course of the development of British education in India. It led also to far-reaching results.

Employment of Grant. One party was in favor of enlarging its previous operations, and of continuing to support and extend Oriental Education, while the other, following the example of Dr. Duff, resolved to prevent such an outlay, and to develop, in its stead, the study of English, as the vehicle for conveying knowledge.

The Controversy. Orientalia *vs.* English. These two parties in the Committee exactly balanced, five against five; but, in point of ability the Orientalists were superior. The controversy was not settled until 1835, when, as we have already said, a stouter champion entered the arena. Lord Macaulay arrived in India in 1834 as the Legislative Member on the Council of the Governor-General. Although appointed President of the Committee, he declined to act until some decision in regard to this bitter controversy was reached. Accordingly, both parties made a final effort and sent in to Government lengthy expositions of their opinions. From his official position on the Supreme Council, Macaulay wrote on the 2d of February, 1835, his celebrated Minute, which Decision. was endorsed by the Governor-General, Lord Bentinck, and was followed on the 7th of March by a proclamation which established the triumph of the English language and of European studies in India. This verdict is the most important fact in the history of English education in India.

Before quoting from the Minute of Macaulay, which was probably the determining argument in the long controversy, and which has now taken rank as an English classic, the Summary of Arguments. arguments on both sides may, with advantage, be summarized.

On the one hand, the Orientalists argued:

Orientalists. 1. That the Act of 1813 provided for the encouragement of the learned natives of India.

2. That Government was, therefore, pledged to keep up its Oriental teaching.

3. That it is unjust to force the people of India to devote themselves to the language of a few foreigners, a language devoid to them of the charm of association and inferior to the ancient literature and thought of their own land.

4. That a thorough Arabic or Sanskrit training was superior to a superficial acquaintance with English.

Anglicists. On the other hand, the advocates of English urged:

1. That even were it granted that by "learned natives" was meant natives learned in Orientalia, yet the act went on to provide for the promotion of a knowledge of the sciences.

2. That Government had never given a distinct pledge to maintain Sanskrit or Arabic studies. Or, if even there existed such a pledge, it had been improperly given, without knowledge of its far-reaching limitations, and the committee was bound to disregard it. By parity of reasoning, instruction based upon new discoveries could not be undertaken.

3. That the Hindus, except a few of the Brahman priests, were themselves in favor of English education, as shown by the success of the Hindu College in Calcutta, and of the college founded by Dr. Duff, in both of which the English classes were much the most popular.

4. That it was not, as was assumed, a question of a superficial knowledge of English, as against a thorough knowledge of Sanskrit or Arabic. The latter were difficult languages, requiring many years for their mastery, while the English was an easy tongue, in which the Hindus had already produced compositions which had excited the admiration of Englishmen.

5. That, finally, a larger view should be taken of all the circumstances. The Hindus had thoroughly explored and

exhausted their early acquired store of knowledge. For many centuries their intellectual position had been that of the schoolmen of Europe. They had sharpened their minds, but had made no progress. Now there was a longing for new information. Was it right to offer them stones when they asked for bread, to turn them back to the "false history, false astronomy, false medicine, and false metaphysics," which attended their false conceptions of life? "It would be as if Europe, at the time of the Renaissance, had been turned aside from their Italian, their Latin, and their Greek, to the Gothic of Ulfilas and the Anglo-Saxon of Beowolf."

Macaulay's Minute, 1835.

And here we may pause to quote some of the most striking paragraphs from Macaulay's Minute:

"It is argued, or rather taken for granted, that by literature, the Parliament can have meant only Arabic or Sanskrit Literature, that they never would have given the honorable appellation of a 'learned native' to a native who was familiar with the poetry of Milton, the metaphysics of Locke, and the physics of Newton; but that they meant to designate, by that name, only such persons as might have studied, in the sacred books of the Hindus, all the uses of cusa-grass, and all the mysteries of absorption into the Deity. This does not appear to be a very satisfactory interpretation. . . . All parties seem to be agreed on one point, that the dialects commonly spoken among the natives of this part of India contain neither literary nor scientific information and that the intellectual improvement of those classes of the people who have the means of pursuing higher studies, can, at present, be effected only by means of some language not vernacular amongst them."

"What, then, shall that language be? One-half of the Committee maintain that it should be English. The other half strongly recommend the Arabic and Sanskrit. The whole question seems, to me, to be which language is best worth knowing?

"I have no knowledge of either Sanskrit or Arabic. But I have done what I could to form a correct estimate of their value. I have read translations of the most celebrated Arabic and Sanskrit works. I have conversed, both here and at home, with men distinguished by their proficiency in the Eastern tongues. I am quite ready to take the Oriental learning at the valuation of the Orientalists themselves. I have never found any one among them who could deny that a single shelf of a good European library was worth the whole native literature of India and Arabia.

"It is, I believe, no exaggeration to say that all the historical information which has been collected from all the books written in the Sanskrit language is less valuable than what may be found in the most paltry abridgments used at preparatory schools in England. In every branch of physical or moral philosophy the relative position of the two nations is nearly the same.

. . . "Whoever knows that language (English), has ready access to all the vast intellectual wealth which all the wisest nations of the earth have created and hoarded in the course of ninety generations. It may safely be said that the literature now extant in that language, is of far greater value than all the literature which, three hundred years ago, was extant in all the languages of the world together.

"Nor is this all . . . It is likely to become the language of commerce throughout the seas of the East. It is the language of the two great European communities which are rising, the one in the South of Africa, the other in Australasia; communities which are every year becoming more important, and more closely connected with our Indian Empire.

"Whether we are looking at the intrinsic value of our literature, or at the particular situation of this country, we shall see the strongest reason to think that, of all foreign tongues, the English tongue is that which would be the most useful to our native subjects."

Lord Bentinck's Proclamation, 1835. This Minute of Lord Macaulay, though containing a prejudiced estimate of Sanskrit literature, remains a model of comprehensive reasoning, and it settled the question so long debated. Its conclusion was endorsed by Lord Bentinck, who issued, in the same year, (1835), a proclamation embodying its principle, and containing the following resolutions:

1. That the chief aim of the educational policy of Government should be to promote a knowledge of European literature and science.

2. That, henceforth, no more stipends should be conferred, but that all existing stipends should be maintained, and all the Oriental Colleges should be continued as long as the natives continued to avail themselves of them.

3. That the printing of Oriental books should at once cease, and

4. That the funds thus set free should be employed in promoting European studies, through the medium of the English language, and that the Committee should at once submit to Government a scheme for effecting this purpose.

Results of the Proclamation. The immediate effect of Lord Bentinck's Proclamation was to put an end to the publication of Oriental books, and to the granting of stipends to students, although some of the latter did not lapse for some time. The direct though more distant results of the Proclamation were the establishment of new schools where English was taught, and the flocking to them of large numbers of students. There was an intellectual stir abroad. Men were eager to learn and to teach. English schools sprang up on all sides. It was said that whereas the Sanskrit Colleges had been almost entirely confined to Brahmans, now Christian, Muhammadan and Hindu boys of every variety of descent might have been seen standing, side by side, in the same class, under the common inspiration of English learning.[1] As an instance, it is recorded that when the Hoogly College was opened in 1836, 1,200 names were enrolled in the first three days; and an auxiliary school was immediately filled. In 1843 there were 51 schools and colleges, containing 8,200 scholars, of whom 5,132 were studying English, 426 Sanskrit, 572 Arabic, and 706 Persian. Such was the effect of substituting English for Sanskrit and Arabic.

Restoration of Funds to Orientalia, 1839. Nevertheless, these languages, while not a suitable medium for general education, were of paramount literary and philological importance, and possessed peculiar claims on the land where they had been so long studied. These claims were too great, indeed, to be entirely neglected, as they bade fair to be at this time. Their claims were again recognized by Lord Auckland in 1839. A Minute of that year restored to Oriental education a considerable grant, Rs. 25,000, which had been alienated from it, and its future became thereby more assured.

The Vernacularists and Anglicists. It was said that Lord Bentinck's Proclamation put to sleep one controversy only to arouse another. This was the controversy between the Vernacularists and the Anglicists; and this was not decided until the end of this period, in 1854.

Mr. Hodgson. During the years 1835–43 the cause of the Vernaculars was championed by Mr. Hodgson, the eminent Sanskritist, who, during his official residency at Nepāl, had discovered so many Buddhist MSS. under the Himalayas. In his opinion, the learned languages had proved a curse to India. The tyranny of the learned class had been perpetu-

[1] Trevelyan. History of Education in India, p. 20.

ated by keeping all knowledge locked up in a sacred language. By this means all the moral effects of knowledge applied to every-day life had been lost. The only remedy that remained, in Mr. Hodgson's view, was to found Normal Schools to train up a body of teachers competent to impart European knowledge through native languages.

Sir Charles Trevelyan. Opposed to this view was that of the Anglicists, led by Sir Charles Trevelyan, who held that the best policy was to push on the English studies and thus create a highly educated class who would in turn spread the desire for knowledge to the class beneath them. While the means at the disposal of the Committee were limited, it was the best course, first, to train up a class of teachers, translators and authors. This was the celebrated "Filtering Down Theory." It was hoped that it would serve as a system of channels for distributing, instead of a dam for confining the waters of knowledge. This was, of course, expecting too much from the expansiveness of European knowledge, but it prevailed at the time.

Councils of Education, 1843. Little now remains to be said concerning Government education during this period. In 1843 "Councils of Education" were created in three Presidencies, to take the place of the former "Committees of Public Instruction." The new body continued the traditional policy of establishing Zillah, or District, Schools.

Government Examinations, 1844. In 1844, Lord Hardinge issued a Proclamation, the object of which was to establish yearly examinations, open to all comers, the results of which would determine Government in the selection of its Civil Servants, a place in it being thus a guarantee of capacity. The total result of this measure was insignificant. In nine years only ten certificated students had obtained offices under Government.

Mr. Thomasen and Village Schools, 1845. In 1845, a plan to encourage native village schools was set on foot by Mr. Thomasen, Governor of the Northwest Provinces. This plan involved the establishment of:

1. An Elementary School for Circles of Villages, each school to be situated in a central village, and no village to be more than one mile from the Central School.

2. A Middle School at the headquarters of each subdivision.

3. A High School in each Zillah, or District.

This plan was sanctioned by the Directors, and a large yearly expenditure of Rs. 500,000 allowed.

1850-4. Operations began in 1850, and by 1854 these schools existed in eight Districts, and had become largely the Educational System of the Province.

Other Provinces. We pass over the development of education in the other Provinces, or Presidencies, in this period, as it does not seem to have resulted in characteristic movements of such importance as to justify our lingering over them.

Missionary Education. It only remains for us to review, briefly, the missionary education of this period. At its close, in the year 1852-53, there were in Government schools about 28,000 children receiving instruction, while, at the same time, the Protestant missionaries were teaching nearly 100,000.[1]

The two systems differed. The two systems differed widely, also, in

(1) Character. The State schools were almost entirely secondary, while the private schools were, to a large extent, primary. It was not true, however, that there was no secondary education carried on by the missionaries. Probably over 12,000 scholars were in their high schools and colleges. Some of the latter, such as the Serampore College, the General Assembly's schools at Bombay and Cal-

[1] Parliamentary Reports for 1852.

cutta, and Dr. Duff's Free Kirk College, were held in very high estimation.

(2) Again, while in Government schools there was no trace of female education, the missionaries were teaching over 13,000 girls.

(3) With regard to the support of these schools, it is claimed that fees were exacted in all State schools, which was not the case in those maintained by missionary societies. This led, naturally, to a distinct difference in the social position of the pupils, so far as wealth was concerned.

General Character of Education. With regard to the general character of the schools during the second period, we may conclude that science was not practically taught, and that in other subjects, while a fair amount was learned, there were no opportunfties for original work, and that the range of examination was too wide to permit reading outside of the set books.

CHAPTER III

Third Period, 1854–82

As the previous period was largely formative in its character, and of great significance because of the initiatory nature of the questions decided, the period under present review is one of organization. The experience and conclusions of the past led to the adoption of a definite system of education, which became a separate department of Government.

Charter of 1853.

In the year 1853 the East India Company's Charter again expired. The customary Lords' Committee was appointed for the purpose of recommending such modifications or additions as might be thought necessary to introduce into the renewed charter. Undoubtedly, the most important of all the subjects which were discussed before this Committee was that of education.

Lords' Committee.

Evidence was taken from such authorities on Indian questions as Sir Charles Trevelyan, the Honorables George Norton and C. H. Cameron, and Drs. Duff, Wilson and Marshman, men who had had long experience in dealing practically with educational questions in the three great Presidencies of Bengal, Bombay and Madras.

Despatch of 1854.

The general results of the evidence taken before the Lords' Committee were compacted and formulated in the Court of Directors' Despatch of 1854, drawn up by Sir Charles Wood, and constituting the great Charter of Indian Education. On that Despatch the whole of the immense system now in existence is based. This document is a long one, extending through 25 finely printed octavo pages. It is of such importance to India in particular, and to students of education in general, that we give here its introductory and concluding paragraphs, and quote *in extenso* an authoritative summary of its contents, as given in the Report of the Indian Education Commission of 1882.

Introduction.

"It appears to us that the present time, when, by an Act of the Imperial Legislature, the responsible trust of the Government of India has, again, been placed in our hands, is peculiarly suitable for the review of the progress which has already been made, the supply of the existing deficiencies, and the adoption of such improvements as may be best calculated to secure the ultimate benefit of the people committed to our charge.

"Among many subjects of importance, none can have a stronger claim to our attention than that of education. It is one of our most sacred duties to be the means, as far as in us lies, of conferring upon the natives of India those vast moral and material blessings which flow from the general diffusion of useful knowledge, and which India may, under Providence, derive from her connection with England. For, although British influence has already, in many remarkable instances, been applied, with great energy and success, to uproot demoralizing practices, and even crimes of a deeper dye, which, for ages, had prevailed among the natives of India, the good results of those effects must, in order to be permanent, possess the further sanction of a general sympathy in the native mind, which the advance of education alone can secure.

"We have, moreover, always looked upon the encouragement of education as peculiarly important, because calculated not only to produce a higher degree of intellectual fitness, but to raise the moral character of those who partake of its advantages, and so to supply you with servants to whose probity you may, with increased confidence, commit offices of trust,[1] in India, where the well-being of the people is so

[1] Public Letter to Bengal, 5th Sept., 1827.

intimately connected with the truthfulness and ability of officers of every grade in all departments of the State."

Conclusion. "We believe that the measures we have determined upon are calculated to extend the benefits of education throughout India; but, at the same time, we must add that we are not sanguine enough to expect any sudden, or even speedy, results to follow from their adoption. To imbue a vast and ignorant population with a general desire for knowledge, and to take advantage of that desire when excited to improve the means of diffusing education amongst them, must be a work of many years, which, by the blessing of Divine Providence, may largely conduce to the intellectual improvement of the mass of the natives of India.

"As a Government, we can do no more than direct the efforts of the people, and aid them wherever they appear to require most assistance. The result depends more upon them than upon us. And, although we are fully aware that the measures we have now adopted will involve, in the end, a much larger expenditure upon education from the revenues of India, or, in other words, from the taxation of the people of India, than is at present so applied, we are convinced that any expense which may be incurred for this object will be amply repaid by the improvement of the country; for the general diffusion of knowledge is inseparably followed by more orderly habits, by increasing industry, by a taste for the comforts of life, by exertion to acquire them, and by the growing prosperity of the people."

Summary of Despatch of 1854. The Summary of the Despatch of 1854, as taken from the Report of the Education Commission, is as follows:

"The Despatch of 1854 commends to the special attention

of the Government of India the improvement and far wider extension of education, both English and vernacular, and prescribes as the means of the attainment of these objects:

1. The constitution of a separate Department of the Administration, for Education.

2. The institution of Universities at the Presidency towns.

3. The establishment of institutions for training teachers, for all classes of schools.

4. The maintenance of the existing Government colleges and high schools, and the increase of their number when necessary.

5. The establishment of new middle schools.

6. Increased attention to vernacular schools, indigenous or other, for elementary education.

7. The introduction of a system of grants-in-aid.

Popular Education.

"The attention of the Government is especially directed to the importance of placing means of acquiring useful and practical knowledge within the reach of the great mass of people. The English language is to be the medium of instruction in the higher branches, and the vernacular in the lower. English is to be taught whenever there is a demand for it, but it is not to be substituted for the vernacular languages of the country.

Grants-in-Aid.

"The system of grants in-aid is to be based on the principle of perfect religious neutrality. Aid is to be given (so far as available funds may render it possible) to all schools imparting a good secular education, provided they are under adequate local management, and subject to Government inspection, and provided that fees, however small, are charged in them.

"No Government colleges or schools are to be founded where a sufficient number of institutions exist, capable with the aid of Government, of meeting the local demand for education; but new schools and colleges are to be established and temporarily maintained where there is little or no prospect of adequate local support being made to meet local requirement. The discontinuance of any general system of education entirely provided by Government, is anticipated with the gradual advance of the system of grants-in-aid; but the progress of education is not to be checked in the slightest degree by the abandonment of a single school to probable decay.

Scholarships. "A comprehensive system of scholarships is to be instituted, so as to connect lower schools with higher, and higher schools with colleges.

Female Education. "Female education is to receive the frank and cordial support of Government.

Government Coöperation. "The principal officials in every district are required to aid in the extension of education; and in making appointments to posts in the service of Government, a person who has received a good education is to be preferred to one who has not. Even in lower situations, a man who can read and write is, if equally eligible in other respects, to be preferred to one who can not."

Despatch of 1859. (Lord Stanley.) Another important educational paper was issued by the India office in 1859, the purpose of which is set forth in its introductory paragraph:

"The time seems to have arrived when some examination may be instituted into the operation of the orders despatched from this country in 1854, for the prosecution of measures on a more extended scale for promoting education in India.

"Such an examination seems more especially required since the measures, and particularly the more recent measures, of Government for the promotion of education have been alleged to be among the causes which have brought about the recent outbreak in the army of Bengal, and the disquietude and apprehension which are believed to have prevailed in some portions of Her Majesty's Indian territories."

Summary.

This Despatch is summarized by the Education Commission of 1882, in its report, in the following terms:

"The second great Despatch on Education, that of 1859, reviews the progress made under the earlier Despatch, which it reiterates and confirms, with a single exception, as to the course adopted for promoting elementary education. While it records with satisfaction that the system of grants-in-aid has been freely accepted by private schools, both English and Anglo-Vernacular, it notes that the native community have failed to co-operate with Government in promoting elementary vernacular education.

Elementary Vernacular Education.

"The efforts of educational officers to obtain the necessary local support for the establishment of vernacular schools, under the grants-in-aid system, are, it points out, likely to create a prejudice against education, to render the Government unpopular, and even to compromise its dignity. The soliciting of contributions from the people is declared inexpedient, and strong doubts are expressed as to the suitableness of the grants-in-aid system, as hitherto in force, for the supply of vernacular education to the masses of the population. Such vernacular instruction should, it is suggested, be provided by the direct instrumentality of the officers of government, on the basis of some one of the plans already in operation for the improvement of indigenous schools, or by any modification of those plans which may suit the circumstances of different Provinces. The expediency of imposing a special rate on the land for the provision of elementary education is, also, commended to the careful consideration of Government."

Special Rates.

Other Despatches.

Other important Despatches, such as those of 1864 and 1866, by Sir Charles Wood and Lord Ripon, respectively, have been issued since 1859. "But the

Dispatches of 1854 and 1859," the Commission states, "stand out from all later documents as the fundamental Codes on which Indian Education rests."

The Subjects. The subjects which we shall now take up, as suggested by these two Despatches of 1854 and 1859 are: The Government Revenue for Education and Grants-in-Aid to the Schools, the Universities and Colleges, and Secondary and Primary Schools. This constituted the organization which was the special work of this period, and which was not completed till its close. But in all essentials, it was contained in these Despatches.

The Revenues. The Revenues are derived from Imperial Grants and Provincial Revenues, Local and Municipal Funds, and Subscriptions and Donations.

Provincial. The Imperial Government has no direct connection with education, and the Provincial Governments are practically autonomous in this as in other respects. Their revenues consist partly of local contributions and partly of an assigned portion of the imperial revenue. The disposal of provincial grants rests entirely with provincial authorities.

Local. The Local Fund taxes are levied by the Provincial Government. The rate differs in the different provinces. It amounts in most provinces to 1 per cent. on the land revenue.

Municipal. The Municipal Fund contributions are to the towns what the local taxes are to the country, since the latter are imposed on land only. About 2½ per cent. of the total revenue is obtained in this way.

Subscriptions and donations include endowments, private subscriptions, and the cost of the missionary and other aided schools above receipts. This amounts to about 17 per cent. of the whole.

Summary. These revenues in 1882 amounted, in all, to Rs. 18,871,501, while in 1853 only Rs. 1,000,000 was spent on education. In the same period the grants had increased in the ratio of one to ten, while the children receiving education had increased in number from 30,000 to 3,000,000.

Grants-in-Aid. Grants-in-Aid were one of the chief features of the Despatch of 1854. It was hoped that with the gradual advance of the system of Grants-in-Aid, the time might come when any general system of education, provided entirely by Government, might be discontinued, and when many of the existing government institutions might be safely closed, or transferred to the management of local bodies under the control of, and aided by, the State.

Rules. Rules for the distribution of this grant were published in 1855 and revised in 1858 and 1865. The conditions of the grant were the admission of the government inspectors, permission to examine the books, accounts, registers, etc.

There was a lack of uniformity in the assignment of the grants, and no less than five systems were in operation.

Salary Grant. The *Salary Grant System*, confined to Madras, was applied only to secondary education. On this system a fixed proportion of the salary of the teacher was contributed by Government in accordance with his general and professional attainments.

Results Grant. The *Results Grants System* was customary in the case of primary education in Madras, and secondary in Bombay. This grant was assigned on the condition of passing the government examinations and was graded to the subject. It had the merit of securing energetic work and of preventing fraud.

Combined Grant. The combined *Salary-Results System*, which insured stability and supplied a motive, was applied to only a few primary schools under local boards.

Fixed Period. The *Fixed Period System* prevailed in almost the whole of Northern and Central India. On this basis an average grant was paid for periods of 3 or 5 years.

Capitative Grant. The *Capitative System* was applied to a few girls' schools in Bengal.

Effects of System. Summarizing the effects of this aided system, we see that the three most important Provinces showed considerable difference. While in Bengal almost all primary education was aided, in Bombay nearly the whole was managed by the department. Again, while in Bombay and Madras instruction was given, directly and indirectly, to about the same number of children, the former had only about 20,000 children in aided schools; the latter, ten times that number.

Results. The results for all India were as follows: 1,150,000 children were in aided primary; 111,000 were in aided secondary schools, the former number representing nearly 57½ per cent.; the latter 53½ per cent. of the total number of children under elementary and secondary instruction, respectively. The total cost to the State was about 18 lakhs of rupees.

In the same year, 1881–82, over 67 lakhs were being expended on the education of 850,000 scholars in State schools and colleges.

Satisfactory. On the whole, therefore, the system of grants-in-aid had proved an immense success. On no other proposed system could such a great extension of range have been effected in so short a time and at so slight an expense. No other system could, by the expenditure of about 18 lakhs per annum, have attracted to the cause of education private contributions in a yearly amount of about 60 lakhs of rupees.

The Universities. As we have already seen, the Despatch of 1854 sanctioned the founding of Universities. The

The Model. model was to be the University of London, as the best adapted to the wants of India, and the one that might be followed with advantage, although some variation would be found necessary in points of detail. The standard required for a degree was to be "such as to command respect, without discouraging the efforts of deserving students." In the competition for honors, "care was to be taken to maintain such a standard as will afford a guarantee for high ability and high attainments; the subjects for examination being so selected as to include the best portions of the different schemes of study pursued at the affiliated institutions."

The Standard.

The Foundation.

Under Acts of Incorporation II., XXII. and XXVII. of 1857, the three Universities of Calcutta, Bombay and Madras were founded. Two other Universities have since been founded: at Punjab, in 1882, and Allahabad, in 1887.

The Senate.

The Universities consist of a Chancellor, the Governor of the Presidency ex-officio, a Vice-Chancellor, and not less than thirty Fellows, who constitute a Senate. The Senates have the management of the funds of the universities, frame regulations, subject to Government approval, under which periodical examinations are held in the different branches of art and science by examiners selected from their own body, or nominated from without by them.

The Faculties.

The Senate is divided into four Faculties, namely, Arts, Law, Medicine and Engineering, and every Fellow belongs to one Faculty at least, and may belong to more than one.

The Syndicate.

The executive government of the University is vested in a Syndicate consisting of the Vice-Chancellor and eight of the Fellows, who are elected for one year by the several Faculties in the following proportions:

Five by the Faculty of Arts.

One by the Faculty of Law.

One by the Faculty of Medicine.

One by the Faculty of Engineering.

Examiners. The Syndicate appoints examiners and regulates examinations; recommends for degrees, honors and rewards; and corresponds on the business of the University.

Boards of Studies. The Syndicate also appoints, from among the Fellows, Boards of Studies in the various branches of knowledge. There were 13 of these Boards in 1892.

Registrar. There is a Registrar appointed by the Senate, who discharges the duties of this office under the instructions of the Syndicate.

Fellows. The Fellows do not correspond to the idea usually associated with the name in Great Britain and America. The office is an honorary one, and is usually conferred on representative, men or upon those who have been active in the cause of education, in any of its branches.

Examinations. In agreement with their London model, the Indian Universities, with the exception of the Punjab, are without a teaching staff, and they confine themselves, for the most part, to holding examinations and granting degrees. The first examination in the Faculty of Arts is that for matriculation at the University. It is about equal in requirements, it is claimed, to the London Matriculation Examination. The subjects of examination are; 1. English. 2. A classical (Oriental or European) or vernacular language. 3. Physics and Chemistry. 4. History, and 5. Geography.

Matriculation.

First in Arts. Those who pass the matriculation examination, if they intend proceeding further, generally enter an affiliated college where they prepare for the *First Examination in Arts*—F. A.—taken in Calcutta and Madras after two years of study from matriculation; or, the Intermediate

Examination in Bombay, Punjab and Allahabad after one year. The subjects are: 1 English, 2 A classical language, (Oriental or European) or a vernacular, 3 Logic, 4 Mathematics, 5 History and Geography, and 6 Physical Science.

Bachelor of Arts. Two years later comes the B. A. examination, which is also similar in standard to that of the London B. A. This has two branches, the Language and the Science Divisions. In the Language Division, the subjects are: 1 English, 2 A classical language (Oriental or European) or a vernacular, 3 Mathematics, and 4 and 5 any two of the following, Moral Philosophy, History and Advanced Mathematics. The Science Division consists of 1 English, 2 Mathematics, 3 Chemistry, 4 Physical Geography, with 5 either Physics, Physiology or Geology.

Master of Arts. The M. A. is an honor examination in Language, Mental and Moral Philosophy, Mathematics, Natural Science or History.

Licentiate in Teaching. In addition to the above, a new examination has recently been instituted for the Degree of Licentiate in Teaching, L. T., in order to obtain which, candidates must have graduated from a university, and must be examined in the Principles and History of Education and Methods of Teaching, and also as to their practical skill in the management of a class, and in teaching.

Law, Medicine, Engineering. The examinations under the Faculties of Law, Medicine and Engineering are on a different footing, and the examinations are open only to those who have passed the first three examinations in Arts, in the case of Law, and the first two in the case of the others. Of the three, the first, Law, attracts by far the largest number of students, and Engineering the least.

The Degrees. The Degrees which are conferred in these differ- different Faculties are:

Bachelor and Master of Arts, and Bachelor of Science.

Licentiate, Bachelor, and Doctor of Medicine.
Licentiate, Bachelor and Master of Civil Engineering.
Licentiate in Teaching, L. T.
Licentiate in Sanitary Science, L. S. Sc.

Their Value. The value of these degrees is fairly uniform in the three older Universities, and on the whole they denote much the same standard of attainments as do those conferred by the University of London. That the standard is as high as the needs of the country require is shown by the large number of those who, content with passing the First Arts examination, fail to proceed to a Degree.

Value of the Universities. In estimating the value of the Universities, we must not lose sight of their original aim. They have not produced, as a rule, great scholars or scientists, although in recent years the University of Bombay has produced a Senior Wrangler at Cambridge, the University of Madras a First Class in the Cambridge Historical Tripos, and the University of Calcutta a scholar who headed the list of the 60 successful competitors in the Civil Service examinations held in England. We have not heard of many great discoveries made by Hindus, although again, in this decade, a Hindu graduate has been receiving the highest honors of the English and French Scientific Societies for the value of his scientific researches. Very few pursue their studies for the love of knowledge, and apart from any mercenary desires. The wealthier classes and the great landed proprietors are scarcely represented. These results, however, the Universities did not, and could not, constituted as they were, aim at effecting. But they have consolidated the education going on throughout the empire, provided examinations requiring a considerable amount of knowledge, and recognized its possession by a degree.

The Colleges. Notwithstanding the absence of an organized instructing agency within itself, the Indian University is more than a mere examining and degree-conferring body. In the By-Laws and Regulations of the Universities, there are "Rules of Affiliation," by means of which Institutions, or Departments of Institutions, may be affiliated to the University in Arts, Law, Medicine, and Civil Engineering.

Affiliation with the Universities.

Arts.

In the Faculty of Arts, institutions are affiliated as Second Grade, or as First Grade Colleges, the former being entitled to enter students for the First Arts examination only, the latter for both the First Arts and the B. A. degree examinations.

Law. Medicine. Engineering.

In the Faculty of Law, affiliated institutions are entitled to enter students for the B. L. Degree examination; in the Faculty of Medicine, for the Medical Degree examinations, and in the Faculty of Civil Engineering for the degree examinations of that profession.

Normal.

Normal institutions are also affiliated and authorized to enter students for the L. T. degree examination.

Conditions.

The conditions of affiliation have reference

(1) To general and professional qualifications of the staff.

(2) To the financial stability of the institution.

(3) To the building and sanitary accommodations; and

(4) The quantity and quality of the furniture and appliances.

Increase.

In 1857, the year of the founding of the Universities, there existed in India 22 arts and two professional colleges. In 1882, the closing year of the period now under review, the number of colleges had increased to 59, thus considerably more than doubling their number in these 25 years. These colleges represent the teaching part of the universities. Their position corresponds to that of the university colleges in relation to the University of London, except as regards the formality of affiliation. In general character, also, it is claimed that they are on a par with these institutions.

Studies. The plan of study is, of course, conditioned by the University examinations, though there are very few, if any, Colleges where all the subjects for the different branches of the B. A. course are taught.

Professors. The Professors and Principals are largely recruited from England, Scotland and America, and, so far as the Government Colleges are concerned, they are subject to frequent transfers. Students. The status and aim of the students are such as have been already described. The only charge on them is for fees, Fees. which vary according to the character of the College, and the class in which they are studying, from Rs. 1 to Rs. 12 per mensem, the highest of which has been held to correspond to a tuition fee of £100 per annum in England.[1] These fees, together with grants, endowments and subscriptions, supply the expenditure on the colleges.

Value of the Colleges. The estimation in which the colleges are held is great. Private study is discouraged, and it is considered very desirable to receive the stamp which the colleges are supposed to impress. Evidence was given before the Commission of 1882 to show that the Colleges and the Universities had tended to raise the moral tone of the commuuity; that the native bench and bar, once the opprobrium of educated India, had acquired a reputation not only for ability, but for trustworthiness; and that the public service was distinguished for intelligence, industry and integrity.

Secondary Education. In 1854, the opening year of this period, there were altogether 107 schools for secondary education. At the conclusion of the period, 1882, the numbers

[1] Sir Roper Lethbridge, High Education in India, p. 107.

had immensely increased, there being 116 Departmental or Government, 174 Aided, and 88 Unaided High Schools, together with 719 Departmental, 1576 Aided and 572 Unaided Middle Schools. Schools for secondary instruction had, therefore, risen from 107 to 3245 within the twenty-five years. The total number of scholars in these schools was, in 1882, about 215,000.

High Schools. The High Schools, owing to their close connection with the Universities, and to their examinations, reached a fairly uniform level. The highest standard attained is that of the University matriculation examination. At this period, in Madras, the Punjab, and the Northwest Provinces, the High Schools contained only the two highest standards. In Bombay they embraced four, while in Bengal every High School was also a Middle and an Elementary School. All of these, however, carried education two years beyond the inferior grade.

Middle Schools. The Middle Schools were of two kinds. Either they were closely connected with the High Schools or they were complete in themselves. The latter was the more common condition. The instruction extended, in most Provinces, over three standards, immediately below the High School. These Middle Schools were again divisible fnto those where English was, and those where it was not taught. The highest standard of education in these schools was represented by the Middle School examination, which included English, a vernacular language, and an Oriental classical language, Mathematics, Geography, History, and Elementary Physical Science.

Secondary schools absorbed about one-fourth of the total expenditure on education, a part being made up of fees, subscriptions and endowments.

Primary Education. Comparing the opening with the closing year of this period, we find in the matter of Primary Education also an enormous increase. In 1854–6 the new Department of Education established under the Despatch of 1857. 1854, received the care of the following pupils:

(1) From the Board of Education of Calcutta, 13,000 pupils.
(2) From the Board of Education of Bombay, 21,400 pupils.
(3) From the Board of Education of Madras, 4,500 pupils.
(4) From the Government of the N. W. P., 24,000 pupils.

Of this total of 63,000 in government schools, probably only a little more than a half, or 35,000 in the whole of India, were receiving a strictly elementary education. In missionary schools primary instruction was being imparted to about 70,000 children in all the provinces.

1882. In the year 1881–82 the elements were being taught in 83,416 public elementary schools of all descriptions, to a total of 2,061,541 pupils.

Methods. It would be perhaps useless and confusing to give the details of this growth in primary education in the different provinces and classes of schools, or the methods by which this enormous increase had been effected. Speaking generally, the methods employed were two; of which one followed in Bengal, aimed at bringing the indigenous schools into more or less close connection with the Department, while the other, prevailing in Bombay, Madras and the remaining provinces, involved a system of local rates. Under the former there was little scope for local management; but of the latter the Local Boards were an essential feature.

Standards. The standards of instruction in the different provinces were diverse, but there were everywhere two examinations, the Upper Primary and the Lower Primary. In general, the former involved reading at sight in the vernacular, writing, some elementary arithmetic Examinations. and a variety of optional subjects, such as history, geography and elementary physics. The Upper Primary examination followed upon the Lower after one year, and added proportionately to these subjects, and in some provinces included a little English. These examinations in 1881–82 were not always compulsory, and in that year only about one-fifth of the total number of scholars of that grade were presented for examination.

Expenditure. Of the total expenditure on primary education, nearly one-third was derived from rates, and about one-fourth from fees, which were, for obvious reasons, very small for primary school pupils.

General Classification. At the end of this period the schools and colleges connected with the Departments of Education were classified as follows:

I. *University Education* was imparted in:

(*a*) First Grade colleges, where the limit of study was the B. A. examination.

(*b*) Second Grade colleges, where the limit of study was the F. A. examination.

II. *Secondary Education* was imparted in:

(*a*) High schools, up to the matriculation examination.

(*b*) Middle schools, up to the middle school examination.

These schools were divided into those in which English was (Anglo-vernacular) and those in which it was not taught.

III. *Primary Education* was imparted in:

(*a*) Upper Primary schools, teaching to the upper primary examination.

(*b*) Lower Primary schools, teaching to the lower primary examination.

This classification was not perfectly carried out everywhere. The gradation was most complete in Bengal and Madras.

Indigenous Schools.

Decrease. The enormous expansion of European education during this period raises the inquiry as to what had become of the indigenous schools. The Government inquiry of 1882 revealed the fact that there were only 350,000 boys receiving instruction in schools of native origin and management, whereas if the proportion of 1830, discovered by the State inquiries of that year, had been maintained, there would have been four times that number, or about 1,500,000.

Reasons. These schools had disappeared in two ways: by absorption and by extinction. In Bengal and Madras, where the growth of primary schools had been effected by the plan of absorption, of ancient native schools, the latter may be said to have still existed in a changed form; but a comparatively small part of the native system was left untouched, so that in Bengal only 60,000 children, and in Madras only 55,000, remained entirely outside of the Department. In the other provinces, where the opposite policy of extinction was followed, the comparatively larger number of native schools represents the whole of what survived.

Differences. An examination of the two systems of State and Indigenous schools will soon reveal their differences, and show the respects in which department schools were better than those they so largely supplanted.

(1) The indigenous schools possessed the tenacity which was peculiar to thoroughly localized institutions, but they were liable to interruption constantly by war or other disturbances.

(2) The modern school was better managed, being liable to inspection, and better taught, since the teacher held a more responsible position, and the curriculum covered a wider range.

(3) The buildings and equipment, generally, were much improved in the modern school.

(4) The exclusion of low-castes and out-castes was discontinued.

The future fate of these indigenous schools is, therefore, likely to be absorption or extinction.

Missionary Education.

At the conclusion of the previous period, 1852, we found that missionary societies were teaching nearly 100,000 children, of whom 28,000 were receiving secondary instruction. At the close of the present period, 1881–2, this total had increased to nearly 200,000, of which number 85,000 boys, and far the larger number of 47,000 girls, belonged to the elementary section. In the 385 colleges and secondary schools maintained by these missionary societies, there were over 45,000 scholars. There is, however, an interesting observation to be made in regard to a decided change in the application of missionary effort to educational work in this period. While less than one-tenth of the number of scholars in aided, and one-twentieth of the total number in primary schools, were in mission schools, about one-third of the number in aided secondary, and about one-sixth of the total number in all secondary schools, were in institutions belonging to missionary societies. The mission colleges had grown to be numerous and important in this period. Some of them, such as the colleges of the General Assembly and Free Church of Scotland at Calcutta, Madras and Bombay, rivalled even the Presidency colleges, with all the resources of the State behind them. The cardinal point of difference between the missionary and the State institutions was that in the one Christianity was, and in the other it was not, taught, although for obvious reasons, the amount of religious instruction given in the former was somewhat restricted. Missionary education had, by the close of this period, taken the third place, in point of numbers, among the agencies for raising the intellectual condition of the Hindus, although, in general efficiency, as well as in expensiveness, the State schools took the lead.

Special Education.

We must close the story of the development of education in this period with a brief account of the state of special education.

Normal Education. Normal education was the subject of a special provision in the Despatch of 1854; and its directions were so far followed that, at the close of this period, nearly one-half of the teachers in Primary Schools under the Department were certificated. But nowhere were there adequate facilities for the training of teachers for Secondary schools, the University examinations supplying, as in Europe and America, at that time, a test of capacity regarded as sufficient.

Technical Education. Technical education was represented by 5 Schools of Art, 18 Engineering Schools and Colleges, and 12 Medical Schools and Colleges. There was no general system of practical, technical or industrial education such as existed in parts of England.

Aboriginal Education. The Aborigines consist of about 6,000,000 of wild Hill tribes, of non-Aryan descent. The difficulty of dealing with these, for obvious reasons, is very great. In 1882, only 13,000 children of these tribes were in schools; and, until very recently the Department had done little to reach them. Missionary societies were at work among them through their schools.

Muhammadan Education. From the earliest days of government education great difficulty had been encountered in prevailing upon the Muhammadan population in India, which is in the proportion of one in five to the whole, to avail themselves of the means of school instruction. This reluctance is partly to be accounted for by the character of their own instruction, which is exclusively religious, with the Koran as the only text-book, and partly by their poverty and their love of the military profession. In 1871 special measures for their education began to be taken. Schools and scholarships were provided for Muhammadans, and Arabic and Persian were encouraged in the universities. To these special schools teachers and inspectors of the same creed were appointed. Everything reasonable, including a fee which was only one-half of that usually demanded of pupils, was done to attract Muhammadans into the schools. But, in 1882, the proportion, while increased, was found to be practically confined to primary schools. A greater progress in Muhammadan education is observed in the provinces where the Musalman population is largest, and during the period following that now under review.

Female Education. Early in the present century the "Union School Society," at Calcutta, turned its attention to the education of women, and opened a school which numbered about 200 girls. In 1824 the "Native Female Education Society" arose, and also founded a school. In 1849 another school for girls was established in Calcutta, where a few girls of high caste were instructed. But the missionaries were the most active in behalf of women, and, in 1851, they had about 13,000 female children under instruction. In 1855 an entirely new scheme was adopted on the initiative of the Rev. W. Forster, a colleague of Dr. Duff. This was the well-known system of Zenana Missions, whereby a number of English ladies formed themselves into societies for visiting Hindu ladies in their homes and giving them instruction. Some of these missions have occasionally received aid from Government for the secular department of this work. In 1881–2 it was calculated that about 9,000 women in all India were being taught on this system at their own homes.

But, apart from these Zenana Missions, there was a system of Government and Aided Schools for girls, similar in character to those for boys. In 1881–2 considerable progress had been made in the various provinces, and, altogether, there were nearly 130,000 girls under instruction, largely in Elementary Schools. But, of the whole number of Hindu girls of school-going age, only .85, or less than one per cent. were at school.

Conclusion.

We have now described, in some detail, the elaborate system of education which was built up during this period of about 25 years, from 1854 to 1881. Except in a few points, the system still remains unchanged. It is a vast machine, which only the persistent efforts of a large number of able men could have succeeded in framing in India. It is not yet complete, but every year adds to its efficiency. Complaints are freely made of a tendency to extreme uniformity. But those who know the immense diversities of opinion and society in native India; those who understand that it is the mission of England to combine separate units into a single whole, and thereby to create a nation out of a congeries of peoples; those who are aware how insignificant is the number of Englishmen who have to direct this immense and ever-increasing body of operations, will not be inclined to deplore a rigor and uniformity which lighten the labor and add to the power of those who govern.

CHAPTER IV

Fourth Period, 1882–98

THIS period has to do with the development of education during the last two decades. It is chiefly concerned with the Education Commission of 1882–3, its inquiries, its conclusions, and the results which have followed.

The chief features of the Despatch of 1854 were the extension of elementary education, and the developmemt of a general plan of education, largely by means of the Grant-in-Aid System. The Government was represented as being "desirous of extending far more widely the means of acquiring general European knowledge of a less high order, but of such a character as may be practically useful to the people of India."[1] It also "looked forward to the time when any general system of education entirely provided by Government might be discontinued with the gradual advance of the system of grants-in-aid."[2]

Attention was, therefore, to be directed to providing education for the mass of the people, "who are utterly incapable of obtaining any education worthy of the name, by their own unaided efforts."[3]

Principles of the Despatch of 1854.

From the above quotations it is evident:

(1) That no addition to the number of Government Colleges was contemplated.

(2) That Sccondary Education was to be left chiefly to the system of Grants-in-Aid.

(3) That attention was primarily to be directed to the education of the great mass of the people.

[1] § 10. [2] § 62. [3] § 41.

These principles were confirmed in the succeeding Despatches of 1859, 1863, and 1871, thus removing any chance for misapprehending the meaning and object of the original Despatch. But notwithstanding the emphasis placed upon these principles, it came to be widely felt, at the beginning of this period, that they had not been adhered to in the administration of education in the different provinces by the Departments organized under the Despatch of 1854.

Departure from these Principles. In 1854–5, the expenditure, from public funds, on education was Rs. 750,000. In 1881–2, it had increased to Rs. 16,000,000. But while in 1854–5 nearly the whole sum came from Imperial Revenues, in 1881–2 about one-fifth was from Local and Municipal Funds. The increase of expenditure contemplated by the Despatch had, therefore, taken place.

But what of its application? At the beginning of the previous period, there were 14 Government colleges, while at the end there were 30 Government, 20 Aided, and 9 Unaided colleges. In regard to the expenditure also, it was found that Government higher education, in 1881–2, was more expensive by Rs. 500,000 than was the whole number of colleges, Secondary and Primary schools in 1854–5. In a total expenditure upon education of Rs. 12,000,000, it was found that Rs. 700,000 was being diverted from Primary and Middle school education for the benefit of High schools and colleges.

Thus there appeared to be an unwarrantable violation of the principles of the Despatch of 1854 to justify, or at any rate, to account for, the wide-spread agitation which began in 1879.

Decrease of Attendance. A still further cause for discontent was found in the comparatively slow increase in the numbers of those under instruction. In 1870–1, there were nearly 1,900,000 children in all the schools; in 1881–2, the number was about 2,650,000, thus showing a yearly increase of about 70,000. The number of children of school age underwent, during this decade, an average annual increase of over 200,-000. Thus British education was shown to be actually falling behind at the rate of 130,000 children every year.

While these may be set down as the chief causes of the movement now gathering force, there were not wanting certain minor causes.

Missionary Representations.

The representatives of missionary bodies, interested in education in India, were active in the agitation from its commencement. Their splendid services to education were too conspicuous to be ignored, or to allow their complaints to go unheeded. They complained of unfair treatment to themselves, in that the Government scholarships were not tenable in their schools, but only in State schools, and that thus the best scholars were attracted away. They were compelled, in some instances, to make use of books of which they entirely disapproved. Unwelcome regulations as to fees, salaries, promotions, were pressed upon them. Their grants were reduced without due notice. The Government inspectors were, not infrequently, unfair to them. There was, naturally, a strong Departmental feeling among the officials, and every possible means was used to support the State schools against rivalry. Although the Despatch of 1854 provided that where an adequate Aided school existed, no State school should be introduced; this regulation, it was claimed, had been repeatedly violated.[1]

General Council on Education in India.

In order, among other reasons, to give strength to these complaints, there was formed, in 1878, in England, the General Council on Education in India, chiefly through the exertions of the Rev. James Johnston, who became the Secretary, as he was the most active member, of the Council. This Council brought the

[1] Answers of Missionaries to questions by the General Council on Education.

movement into notice. It contained such names as the Earl of Shaftesbury, Lord Lawrence, and even Sir Charles Wood, the author of the great Despatch of 1854. Pledges were secured from those in authority that an inquiry would be instituted as to the carrying out of the principles of the Despatch.

Defense of System. On the other side was ranged nearly the whole body of the officials and professors connected with the Department, along with a large proportion of educated Hindus. In answer to the complaints made, no attempt seems to have been made to invalidate the facts urged, concerning the actual state of distribution of educational efforts and funds. Indeed, an effort was made to show that the Despatch of 1854 did not forbid a development of high education carried on by the State.[1] But, in the face of the quotations cited, this could not stand. The argument upon which the greatest reliance was placed was known as the "Filtering down theory," namely, that it was necessary, first, to create a highly educated class, by which means general education would be, in the end, more quickly and more surely conveyed to the masses.

As against the missionary party, it was asserted that they were at the bottom of the whole agitation, and that, being unable to sustain competition with the Department, they desired to rid themselves of their rival, and thus to be relieved of the necessity of making the strenuous efforts now forced upon them. It was asserted that the missionaries desired to get the whole of the higher education in their hands, after which the standards would be lowered, and everything taught would be with religious and sectarian bias.

The sufficient answer to this charge lay in the demand, not that the State colleges should be abolished, or placed in the hands of missionaries, but that they should be transferred

[1] High Schools in India, Sir Roper Lethbridge.

to local bodies, consisting mainly of Hindus, the men who required to be protected from the missionaries.

Appointment of the Commission.

Such was the state of the controversy when, on the 3d of February, 1882, the Government of India appointed an Education Commission, with a view to inquiring into the working of the existing system of Public Instruction, and to the further extending of the same system, on a popular basis. The Commission consisted of twenty-one members, under the Presidency of Sir William W. Hunter, LL.D., C. I. E., a member of the Viceroy's Legislative Council, a high authority on all Indian affairs, and, in every way, fitted to preside over this important inquiry. Associated with him were men representative of the official, missionary and native views, and also of the different races and classes interested in Education in India.

Instructions.

In the instructions accompanying the appointment, the Government observed that "owing to a variety of circumstances, more progress has, up to the present time, been made in high and middle than in primary education. The Government of India is not disposed, in any way, to regret this advance. But the Government holds that the different branches of public instruction should, if possible, move forward together, and with more equal step than hitherto, and the principal object, therefore, of the inquiry of the Commission should be, 'the present state of elementary education throughout the Empire, and the means by which this can, everywhere, be extended and improved.'"

The Commission was, at the same time, instructed to inquire into the possibility of a wider extension of the Grant-in-Aid System, in connection with high and middle education. The best way of securing the aid of local and municipal bodies, in the management of public schools, was also to be considered. The Commission was also directed to "particularly inquire as to the extent to which indigenous schools exist in different parts of the country, and are, or can be, utilized as a part of the educational system." With regard to secondary education, the Commission was directed to inquire "into the quality and character of the instruction imparted in schools of this elass." The important subject of female education was also to receive special attention, and the best means of encouraging and extending it were to be considered.

Proceedings of Commission. Such was the wide scope of the inquiry entrusted to this Commission. It met at Calcutta soon after appointment, on the 10th of February, 1882, and sat regularly, preparing a scheme of operations and examining the local witnesses. For the following eight months, the President, Dr. Hunter, visited the different provinces, collecting material, receiving petitions, and examining witnesses. A very wide-spread interest was aroused on the subject of education. Large meetings were held to welcome the Commission or its representatives. Nearly two hundred memorials were presented, about half of them coming from educational societies and municipal and other public bodies. When the Commission assembled again in Calcutta on the 5th of December, 1882, an immense mass of evidence had been collected. Over three months were spent in digesting this by means of sub-committees, and in arriving at no less than 222 Resolutions, 180 of which were carried unanimously. On the 16th of March, 1883, the Commission concluded its collective labors, leaving the preparation of the report to a committee of five members, representing the different provinces, and the President. The report is a folio volume of 600 pages. After an introductory review of education in India, it devotes separate chapters to the special subjects of reference.

Recommendations of the Commission. These subjects were: Indigenous, Primary, Secondary, and Collegiate education, the education of classes requiring special treatment, the administration of the Department, and educational legislation. The whole concludes with a recapitulation of the recommendations made.

We are here not so much concerned with a complete historical record as with a recognition of the paramount and characteristic tendencies and achievements of each period. Our purposes are, therefore, met by a brief statement of the principal recommendations of the Commission.

Indigenous Education. After a brief survey of indigenous education in India, its distinctive features, and the status of the teachers in such schools, it is recommended: "That all indigenous schools, whether high or low, be recognized and encouraged if they serve any purpose of secular education."

"That special encouragement be afforded to indigenous schoolmasters to undergo training."

"That a steady and gradual improvement be arrived at, with as little immediate interference with the personnel and curriculum of indigenous schools as possible."

Primary Education. Based upon the policy of the Despatch of 1854, it was natural that much attention should have been given to the subject of primary education. The Commission emphasized the point that elementary instruction was to be regarded as an end in itself, and not necessarily as a portion of the instruction leading up to higher education; and it was recommended:

"That, while every branch of education can justly claim the fostering care of the state, it is desirable, in the present circumstances of the country, to declare the elementary education of the masses to be that part of the educational system to which the strenuous efforts of the state should now be directed in a still larger measure than before."

A uniform standard of examinations was laid down for Primary schools, the standards being so revised as to include more practical subjects, as native arithmetic, mensuration, and elementary physics. The method of assigning aid was to be that of payment by results, the funds to be drawn from local revenues.

Secondary Education. Secondary education, as the term is understood in India, was described, in general terms, by the Commission as "that which leads up from the primary to the collegiate course." It was pointed out that while the higher limit was precisely defined by the matriculation standard of the Universities, the starting point, in secondary education necessarily varied with the varying limits of primary instruction, as that was understood in the different provinces. With regard to Secondary schools, it was distinctly laid down: "That the relation of the State to secondary is different from its relation to primary education, in that the means of primary education may be provided without regard to the existence of local coöperation, while it is ordinarily expedient to provide the means of secondary education only where adequate local coöperation is forthcoming." It was, therefore, recommended that Secondary schools for instruction in English be established thereafter by the State, preferably on the system of grants-in-aid. The certificate of having passed the final examinations in these schools was to be accepted, in the judgment of the Commission, as a general test of fitness for the public service.

Collegiate Education. Some of the important subjects dealt with in this chapter of the report are the scope and character of collegiate instruction, the salaries and status of professors, etc. The question of Government connection with the colleges was to be adjusted by dividing them into three classes: (1) Those from which it would be premature to withdraw. (2) Those which might, with advantage, be transferred to local native bodies. (3) Those which might be transferred, without condition, to local bodies, or be closed altogether.

Among the recommendations of the Commission on Collegiate education were the following:

That Indian graduates be more largely employed than they have hitherto been in State colleges.

That an attempt be made to prepare a moral text-book, based upon the fundamental principles of natural religion.

That the principal, or a professor, in each government and aided college deliver to each of the college classes a series of lectures on the duties of a man and a citizen.

Educational Legislation.

The system of Local Boards, which undoubtedly affected the conduct and character of education in India more than any other recommendation of the Commission, was the subject of very considerable discussion, and, perhaps, the most important suggestions were those which concerned these school boards. Local Boards, with varying powers, and a varying amount of control over primary education, existed in all the provinces. Their duties were, now, to be more clearly defined by provincial enactments. The school district was to become identical with any municipal or rural unit of local self-government. All schools in the district, Department and Aided, were to be placed under the school boards, with the distinct proviso, however, that it should be open to the Provincial Government to exclude any schools, or class of schools, not primary, from their control, and that the managers should not have their existing powers curtailed except by authority of the Provincial Government. The conduct of the Boards was to be regulated by codes defining their relations to the Department, and the scope, function and rules of the system of grants-in-aid. Their funds were to be drawn from an assignment of provincial revenues, and from a fixed proportion of local and municipal funds.

Reception of the Report.

Such are the main features of the recommendations submitted by the Education Commission. They were the result of very extensive investigations, lengthy discussions, and many compromises and concessions. In the final stage they were, however, passed with singular unanimity, and were everywhere favorably received.

Government Action.

A resolution[1] of the Imperial Government approved all the more important recommendations, rejecting the suggestions concerning the 'moral text-book,' and the college lectures on 'the duties of a man and a citizen.' After the report had been adopted the question remained as to what reception it would meet from Provincial Governments. All were well-disposed, as it proved. Bengal declared its intention of increasing its annual expenditure, in regular gradations, through a given number of years. In Madras five per cent. of the provincial revenue was to be permanently assigned to education. Similar arrangements were to be effected in other provinces, except in the Punjab, where the Government declared its inability to increase its expenditure on education.

By 1886–7 the total expendure was Rs. 25,500,000 as agains Rs. 16,000,000 in 1881–2. In the former year, Rs. 8,600,000 came from Government, and Rs. 4,900,000 from local sources, while in the latter, Rs. 7,500,000 were contributed by Government, and only Rs. 3,200,000 by local bodies. In the decade from 1878–1888 the total increase was over Rs. 10,000,000.

The progress made in certain important particulars appears from the Tables below. While the general character of the system has not greatly altered since 1882, there have been some changes in proportions and distributions. The greatest of the administrative changes—the formation of Local Boards—is destined to have more than educational consequences.

The following Tables illustrate the progress made in edu-

[1] October 25, 1884.

cation since the report of the Education Commission in the direction of attendance, revenue and expenditure.[1]

PUPILS.

Year.	*Primary Schools.*	*Secondary Schools.*	*Colleges.*
1881–2	2,061,541	214,164	5,897
1891–2	2,837,607	473,294	16,277
1896–7	3,209,825	535,155	18,783

PUPILS.

Year.	*Aided Schools.*	*Unaided and Private Schools.*
1881–2	1,352,853	361,768
1891–2[1]	1,765,626	969,241
1896–7[1]	2,019,800	1,100,582
[1] Increase	14 per cent.	14 per cent. = 14 per cent.

REVENUES.

Year.	*Prov. Funds.* Rs.	*Local Funds.* Rs.	*Munic. Funds.* Rs.	*Fees.* Rs.	*Other Sources.* Rs.
1881–2	7,392,680	2,952,567	457,436	4,392,664	3,876,154
1891–2[1]	8,813,549	5,394,808	1,409,827	8,854,750	6,046,698
1896–7[1]	9,522,985	5,745,944	1,496,721	10,610,933	7,868,317
[1] Increase	8 p. c.	7 p. c.	6 p. c.	20 p. c.	30 p. c. = 15 p. c.

EXPENDITURES.

Year.	*Universities.* Rs.	*Colleges.* Rs.	*Second'y Educ.* Rs.	*Prim'y Educ.* Rs.
1881–2	177,740	1,681,103	4,380,000	8,200,000
1891–2[1]	473,142	2,872,833	9,895,691	9,614,284
1896–7[1]	670,895	3,270,288	11,452,219	11,088,854
[1] Increase	42 per cent.	14 per cent.	16 per cent.	15 per cent. = 22 per cent.

[1] Second and third Quinquennial Reports on The Progress of Education in India, 1878–88 to 1891–92, 1892–93 to 1896–97.

CHAPTER V

B. *Present Condition of Education in India*

WE confine ourselves in this section to a brief résumé of the present condition of education in India, bringing our review down to 1897, as the last authoritative statement issuing from the Imperial Government was contained in the Third Quinquennial Review of the Progress of Education in India, covering the period 1892–3 to 1896–7, the official year commencing with April 1st.[1]

I. *The Steps* leading to the establishment of the present system of education in India have been four:

a. Lord Macaulay's Minute of 1835.

Leading to a determination of the issue between European learning and the English language, as against Oriental learning and the Classical languages of India.

b. The Court of Directors' Despatch of 1854.

Being the great charter of education in India and outlining the present organization.

c. The Universities Acts of Incorporation of 1857.

Establishing the great Indian Universities of Calcutta, Madras and Bombay.

d. The Education Commission of 1882.

Reviewing the past, and confirming that which

[1] The Reports on Public Instruction in the various provinces for 1897–8, together with the Resolution of the Government of India thereon, have recently appeared. Owing to the presence of abnormal conditions throughout India during the year, the prevalence of famine and the bubonic plague, there was a perceptible decrease in most of the returns for education in India in that year. It seems, therefore, best to draw our figures from the last Quinquennial Review, 1892–3 to 1896–7, as covering a normal period, and as supplying a better basis for our comparisons and conclusions.

had been found most useful in experience and most needed in order to the conferring of the benefits of education upon the great mass of the people.

II. *Organization :*

a. Classification of Institutions.[1]

1. Public Institutions.
   (*a*) Government Schools.
   (*b*) Private-Aided Schools.
2. Private Institutions.
   Private Unaided Schools.

- University Education.
  - Arts Colleges.
    - First Grade.
    - Second Grade.
  - Professional Colleges.
    - Law.
    - Medicine.
    - Engineering.
    - Agriculture.
    - Teaching.
- School Education.
  - General.
    - Secondary.
      - High Schools.
      - Middle Schools.
    - Primary.
      - Upper Primary.
      - Lower Primary.
  - Special.
    - Schools of Medicine.
    - " " Engineering.
    - " " Surveying.
    - " " Agriculture.
    - " " Art.
    - " " Commerce.
    - " " Industries.
    - " " Teaching.

[1] Madras Educational Rules, 1891.

b. Recognition of Institutions.[1]

Based upon

1. Head Master and Staff. Their qualifications, general and professional.
2. Accommodation and Sanitation.
3. Observance of Inter-School Rules.
4. Maintenance of School Registers.
5. Conformity to Rules of Discipline.

c. Grants-in-Aid.[2]

1. Salary Grants—one-half, one-third, one-fourth, acccording to qualfications.
2. Results Grants—per capita, according to examnation results.
3. Scholarship Grants—one-half.
4. Building Grants—one-third.
5. Furniture and Library Grant—one-half.
6. Endowment Grants—one-half.

III. *Administration.*

a. University Education.[3]

1. Senate: Chancellor, Vice-Chancellor, and Fellows.
2. Syndicate: Vice-Chancellor and eight Fellows.
3. Faculties: Arts, Law, Medicine, Engineering.
4. Boards of Studies: Thirteen branches of knowledge.
5. Examiners: Twenty-six subjects of examination.
6. Registrar: Executive officer.

Degrees: B. A., M. A., B. L., M. L., L. M. S., B. M. and M. S., M. D., C. E., L. T.

Honorary: LL.D.

[1] Madras Educational Rules, 1891.

[2] Madras Grant-in-Aid Code, Revised 1897.

[3] Madras University Calendar, 1892.

b. School Education.[1]

1. Director of Public Instruction—Province.
2. Inspector and Inspectress—Circles.
3. Assistant Inspectors—Divisions.
4. Sub-Assistant Inspectors—Districts.
5. Inspecting School Masters—Taluks.

c. Special Education.[1]

1. Schools for Teachers.
2. " Girls.
3. " Muhammadans.
4. " Panchammas, or non-caste pupils.
5. " Aboriginal Tribes.
6. " Native Chiefs and Nobles.
7. " Industries and the Arts.
8. " Oriental Literature.

IV. *Statistics.*[1]

Population of India:[2]

Hindus	207,000,000
Muhammadans	57,000,000
Buddhists	7,000,000
Christians	2,250,000
Others	13,500,000
Total	286,750,000

Area covered by Educational Tables:

Square miles	1,074,268
Population	232,490,022
Period	1892-3 to 1896-7

Estimated population of school-going age = 15 per cent.

NOTE—Except where otherwise stated, these figures are for 1896-97, the last year of the Quinquennial Period.

[1] Education in India, Third Quinquennial Review, 1892-3 to 1896-7.
[2] Census of India, 1891.

a. Number and Attendance.

1. Institutions and Pupils in all India.

Public Institutions	109,886	Pupils	3,788,382
Private Institutions	42,139	Pupils	568,488
Totals	152,025		4,356,870
Increase over 1891-2	7 p. c.		13 p. c.

2. Proportion of Institutions to Towns and Villages.

	For Males.	*For Females.*	*Total.*
	25.08	1.39	26.47
Increase over 1891-2	2.24	0.25	2.49

NOTE: Excluding cities, 3 villages out of 4 still without schools.

3. Proportion of Pupils to School-going age = 15 per cent.

	Males.	*Females.*	*Totals.*
Attendance	3,954,712	402,158	4,356,870.
Percentage	22.3	2.3	12.5

4. Institutions and Pupils according to Class of Institutions.

	Institutions.	*Pupils.*
Colleges	160	18,783
Secondary Schools	5,267	535,155
Primary Schools	103,920	3,209,825
Special Schools	539	24,619
Private Schools	42,139	568,488
Totals =	152,025	4,356,870
Increase over 1891-2	7 p. c.	13 p. c.

5. Institutions and Pupils according to Management.

	Institutions.	*Pupils.*	*Proportion.*
State	22,286	1,236,488	28.4
Aided	63,955	2,019,800	46.4
Unaided	23,645	532,094	12.2
Private	42,139	568,488	13.0
Totals	152,025	4,356,870	100.0

6. Pupils according to Race or Creed:

	Pupils.	Increase over 1891–2.	In total Population.	Percentage of Pupils.
European and Eurasian.	29,176	13 p. c.	.09	3.18
Native Christian.......	114,695	18 "	.55	5.16
Hindus	2,935,597	13 "	71.29	72.86
Muhammadans........	966,632	13 "	21.81	14.62
Others	310,770	7 "	6.26	4.18
Totals..........	4,356,870	13 p. c.	100.00	100.00

7. Pupils according to Languages learned:

	English.	Per Cent.	Classical Languages.	Per Cent.	Vernaculars.	Per Cent.
Public Institutions..	433,606	11.4	302,482	7.9	3,670,362	97
Private Institutions .	5,240	...	268,727	..	328,840	
Totals	438,846		571,209		3,999,202	

NOTE.—1 in 79 of school-going age learning English.

b. Expenditure.[1]

1. Expenditure on Education according to Sources:

	Rs.	Increase over '91–2.
Provincial Funds................	9,522,985	8 p. c.
Local Funds....................	5,745,944	7 "
Municipal Funds................	1,496,721	6 "
Fees	10,610,933	20 "
Other Sources..................	7,868,317	30 "
Totals	35,244,900	15 p. c.

2. Expenditure from Public and Private Funds:

Pubilc funds	Rs. 16,917,552	48 p. c.
Private funds................	18,327,348	52 "
Totals	Rs. 35,244,900	100 p. c.

[1] About Rupees three to one Dollar.

3. Expenditure according to Institutions.

	Rs.	Increase over '91–2.
Universities	670,895	42 p. c.
Colleges	3,270,288	14 "
Secondary Schools	11,452,219	16 "
Primary Schools	11,088,854	15 "
Special Schools	1,927,376	13 "
Direction and Inspection	2,437,337	8 "
Scholarships	797,738	10 "
Building and Furniture	2,370,127	9 "
Miscellaneous	1,230,066	55 "
Totals	Rs. 35,244,900	15 p. c.

4. Average Cost of each Pupil, according to Grade.

Colleges—Arts	Rs. 160.3 per year.
Colleges—Professional	196.4 " "
Secondary Schools	27.7 " "
Primary Schools	3.4 " "
Training Schools	131.1 " "
Special Schools	63.7 " "
General Average	Rs. 96.1

5. Average Cost of each Pupil, according to Management.

State Schools	Rs. 85 per year.
Aided Schools	69 " "
Unaided Schools	30 " "
General Average	Rs. 61

c. Special Educatton.

1. Training Schools.

		Increase over '91–2.
For Masters, Schools	141	22 p. c.
" " Pupils	4,607	4 "
" Mistresses, Schools	45	22 "
" " Pupils	1,118	41 "

2. Technical Schools.

	1896–7.	*1891–2.*
Engineering, Schools	33	28
" Pupils	2,060	1,526
Industrial, Schools	57	69
" Pupils	3,101	3,860
Art, Schools	6	6
Art, Pupils	1,398	1,048

3. Girls' Schools.

Public Institutions	Girls	360,006
Private "	Girls	45,152
Total		402,158
Percentage of school age		2.34

According to Race or Religion, and Stage of Instruction.

	Hindus.	*Muham-madans.*	*Native Christians.*
Secondary, English	5.6	.1	27.8
" Vernacular	63.6	4.1	29.1
Primary	71.9	21.8	.6
Average	47.	8.7	19.3
In total population	71.3	21.8	.6

4. Oriental Education.

		Pupils.
Colleges	5	487
Schools, Sanskrit	2,484	29,060
" Arabic or Persian	2,647	35,578
" Other Oriental Classics	49	744
Totals	5,185	65,869

d. Examinations:

1. University. Quinquennium, 1892–3 to 1896–7.

Examination.	*Candidates.*	*Passed.*	*Per Cent.*	*1887–8 to 1891–2.*
First Arts	31,287	12,425	39.7	34.2
B. A., etc	14,213	6,223	43.8	43.5
M. A., etc	1,239	569	45.9	45.0
Law	5,624	2,241	39.8	46.7
Medicine	3,655	1,755	48.0	46.4
Engineering	2,712	1,502	55.4	47.0

2. Matriculation.

Quinquennium, 1893–97..	Candidates, 76,689	Passed, 30,979	40.4
Year, 1896–97	" 17,952	" 7,916	43.8

3. Primary.

Year, 1896–97	Candidates, 395,158	Passed, 243,820	62.0

CHAPTER VI

C. *A Discussion of Some of the More Important Problems Connected with Education in India.*

THE story which we have attempted, in the preceding pages, briefly to record, of the development of the modern British system of education by superimposing it upon the ancient, indigenous system, so long-lived and so wide-spread in India, gives rise to many interesting inquiries. To those who are within, and who are personally concerned with the introducing of the new and with the conserving of that which is useful of the old, serious questions have been presented, as numerous as they are perplexing. For these men, and for the splendid courage and fine spirit they have shown in meeting their heavy responsibilities, and in carrying forward so successfully their stupendous task of putting new wine into old bottles without doing too great violence to either, the writer, after a personal experience with them, and a knowledge of their achievements, extending over a number of years, has only the profoundest respect and the greatest admiration.

Questions of Indian Administration.

From the standpoint, however, of the educational historian, who is studying from without this striking experiment, whereby the newest European methods are being applied to the reorganization of a long stationary Asiatic society, and who is looking for the lessons that may be useful in the development of his own expanding national life, there are still larger problems of vital significance in their application to new and widening responsibilities.

Problems of National Development.

To these larger problems we will confine ourselves in this concluding chapter.

Current Discussions. The two most important and authoritative contributions that have been made to current discussions upon these educational problems in India, are the recent editorial utterances of the London *Spectator*, under the title, "Three Rotten Cultures,"[1] and the Chancellor's address, delivered at the recent Allahabad University Convocation, in March, 1899.[2] The former is a very severe criticism of the results of British education upon the development of culture in India, while the latter is an admirable summing up of the present educational situation in India, presenting with discrimination the advantages that have accrued to that country from the introduction of that system, without attempting to minimize the defects that experience has discovered in it.

In order to a thorough understanding of the merits and demerits of the present educational system in India, and of its points of defence and attack, we shall make liberal use of these two statements.

"Three Rotten Cultures." The editor of *The Spectator* defines his "Three Rotten Cultures" to be, the Culture of Rome, as it existed during its period of decadence, when the barbarians were breaking up the empire, which culture he calls the education of Roman Nobles; the Culture of the Chinese *Literati*, the feeding upon a few classics and nothing else, which he characterizes as the education of the Chinese Mandarins; and then he proceeds to a description of the third, as follows:

"For the other culture, of nearly the same kind, we are ourselves responsible. It is that of the graduates of Bombay and Bengal. We are taking, yearly, thousands of Mahrattas and Bengalees, who are, naturally, among the most

[1] *The Spectator*, March 18, 1899.

[2] *The Educational Review of India*, April, 1899.

intelligent of mankind, and are setting them to learn the masterpieces of English literature. In a way they do learn them, as the Roman nobles learned their classics; that is, they learn their words without imbibing one particle of their spirit. They devote the whole power of most acute minds to acquiring just so much knowledge of English ideas as will enable them to pass for a degree. The degree once obtained, they are, they think, cultivated men, and put forward their claim to all official posts, as did also the Roman nobles, and are proud, as they were, of the distance between themselves and the uninstructed vulgar. Like them they are indifferent to science and the constructive arts; like them, they seem to have, in politics, no sort of efficiency; like them, they are disposed to tolerate corruption, if only the corrupt have both culture and what they consider manners . . .

"We do not think, as so many do, that they will become formidable to our rule; but we do think that, in educating them on so false a system, we have made the second great blunder of our rule—the first is closing too many careers—and have diffused, instead of the light, a mere imitation of it. We have, too, made a very respectable class permanently unhappy. The graduates are unfitted for any careers except in Government offices, and for every three of these there is, now, but one appointment. By and by there will be a terrible amount of latent, thoughtful disaffection. Whether there is any remedy, we are not certain. To abandon, at once, an experiment so vast as the secular education of a continent, while its subjects warmly approve it, is a daring undertaking, from which even a Government like that of India may reasonably shrink. But of this we do feel certain, that education in India, as hitherto pursued, is of no more value than the education of nobles in the late Roman period, or of Chinese mandarins now, and, like theirs, will ultimately fall, probably with a crash."

The Allahabad University Convocation Address, 1899.

In the Allahabad University Convocation Address, the Chancellor, Sir Antony MacDonnell, reminds us that not until the results of discussions and experiments were summed up in Sir Charles Wood's great educational Despatch of 1854, was the true path of progress marked out, and that since then there has been steady progress along that path. Even the storm of the mutiny, which followed so soon after, and which, for a time, overthrew all order, was powerless to stem the rising tide of educational development along the line of a high ideal, that of "conferring upon the natives of India those vast moral and material blessings which flow from the general diffusion of useful knowledge, and which India may, under Providence, derive from her connection with England." As the Chancellor claimed, there is nothing more honorable to the race, or more becoming to the cause of education, than the fact that, while the storm of fanaticism and ignorance was at its height, the administrators of India set themselves, with calmness and deliberation, to pursue the policy of establishing Universities, and an Educational System, thus creating that knowledge which, alone, can exorcise the spirit of fanaticism from which India was suffering.

Gains to the Credit of the Educational Department.

In regard to the gains which can be placed to the credit of the educational department of the provinces, the Chancellor stated that they were of two kinds: "Gains to the public and to the promoters of commercial and industrial enterprise in the country, by the provision of trustworthy and efficient public officers, agents, and servants of all classes; and gains to the public, generally, in the establishment of better intellectual, social, and moral standards." He claimed with the added authority of one who had had administrative experience, as Lieut.-Governor of the North West Provinces, that a vast improvement had been effected in the purity and efficiency of the administration, by the introduction into it of the men turned out by the schools and colleges of the country. He then quotes the opinion of the Education Commission, that "throughout the country civil officers have begun to discover and readily to acknowledge that in integrity, capacity for work, intelligence and industry, the subordinate trained in college excels his fellows brought in in accordance with the traditions of the past. At the Bar the students of our colleges acquit themselves with distinguished success, and their influence has been generally of a healthy kind. When command of capital opens to them a commercial career, the general testimony is of the same purport as that borne to the credit with which they fill other positions in life." Sir Antony MacDonnell adds with emphasis: "That was the opinion of the Education Commission fifteen years ago; in my judgment, and I speak from experience of administrative control in four out of the eight great provinces of the Empire, *it is truer now than it was then.* This improvement of the moral standard in the public service and in professional and commercial life, manifests itself in many ways. Of all these ways, perhaps the most interesting and hopeful lies in the better conception of duty and responsibility which is spreading, in the attentive and reverent respect now being paid to the purer ethics of the earlier creeds, and in the efforts being made to purify caste customs and rites of their extravagances. These are great gains; they are progressive and cumulative, and they should not be forgotten by any one who undertakes to weigh our educational endeavors in the balance."

Education Commission on the Improvements of Graduates.

All impartial students of education in India must admit that this calm and deliberate testimony from those who have made careful inquiries and have had long experience, goes far to refute the charge of *The Spectator*, that the educational system in India "does not alter the character or enlarge the abilities."

The Testimony of Facts.

This, then, is the testimony of painstaking investigation and of large experience, in contravention of the parallelism drawn between the English-speaking graduate and the Roman noble of the period of decadence, and the Chinese *literati*, or mandarins, of the present. But what is the testimony of facts?

Principal Miller of Madras.

This has been supplied for us in a calm, dispassionate, and convincing statement, called forth by the criticism of *The Spectator*, from Principal William Miller, for many years a leading member of the Senate of the Madras University, a potent voice in the Education Commission of 1882, and, for over three decades, a determining influence in every department of educational activity in the Presidency of Madras, if not in the whole of India. No individual, not excepting Government officials, has had a greater power in the moulding and directing of education in India in recent times. Viceroys have made willing acknowledgment of the indebtedness of the Government of India to this veteran missionary educationist, and among the letters called forth by *The Spectator's* article was one from a former Governor of the Madras Presidency, who based his reply largely upon the character and achievements of Dr. Miller.[1] A worthy successor of Dr. Duff, of Calcutta, and Dr. Wilson, of Bombay, Dr. Miller has long been Principal of the Madras Christian College, the most popular and successful, if not also the best equipped collegiate institution in all India. The testimony of such a witness, and drawn from such a source, must be well-nigh conclusive.

In his reply to *The Spectator*,[2] Dr. Miller gives an analysis of the careers followed by the 880 graduates of the Madras Christian College, admitted to be an important and representative institution, between the years 1869 and 1894.

[1] *The Spectator*, May 27, 1899. [2] May 20, 1899.

Dr. Miller on Proportion of Graduates in Government Service.

"Of the 880, those in the employment of the British Government number 390. Meanwhile, 430 are known to be following careers outside of the service of the Government. Of those in independent employment, 160 are making their way in the world as lawyers. More than 100 are principals, professors, tutors, or teachers in non-Government colleges or schools. About 80 are employed in different capacities by local bodies and native noblemen. Some, though far too few, are traders or contractors on their own account. A few attend to the cultivation of their own lands. Some are engineers, medical practitioners, editors of newspapers, or are employed by banks and railways. Again, of the 880 graduates, 30 are Christians, of whom a third are in the service of the Government, and two-thirds are otherwise employed.

"Of the 390 who are employed by Government, it is true that the large number of 180 are clerks or accountants in government offices. These are, chiefly, the younger men. But government service affords many different careers. Thus less than half of those employed by the State, and much less than a quarter of the whole number of our graduates, are in 'Government offices.' Scores of those in State employment are magistrates, revenue officers, and registrars. Many are professors, or lecturers in Government colleges. Government service may mean much besides clerical work in an office. Does it not seem as if there were nearly as much variety of career among our graduates as among educated men at home?"

Position of Indian Graduates.

Dr. Miller goes on to assert that among the thousand graduates of his own college and the hundreds of graduates from other colleges, he has found but little of that discontent with everything except an official career. On the contrary, he claims to have found among them a growing amount of healthy readiness to set their hands to any useful work. Whether the India graduates are "unfitted" for the careers on which they enter is a large question. Doubtless they might be better fitted than they are. Still, it is believed on all sides that the standard of honesty and efficiency in the public service and in all kinds of work in which educated men engage in India, has risen greatly. Testimony to this effect has frequently been borne by those best qualified to judge, as we have already seen. "It will be universally admitted," says Dr. Miller, "that in India men of some culture show a greater preference than is healthy for employment under Government. Other defects may easily be detected in Indian graduates. There are defects, too, in those who instruct them and in the system under which they work. But even in Britain and elsewhere, graduates, and their instructors and the systems of education, come far short of perfection."

Dr. Miller does not deny that there are many defects in Indian education. "Still, it seems to me," says he, in his letter to *The Spectator*, "that these well-ascertained facts point to somewhat different conclusions from those at which you arrive in your article on 'Three Rotten Cultures.'"

This position of Dr. Miller, and of many others agreeing with him, received high official confirmation in the Convocation Address of Madras University in 1895, when the Governor of Madras, as Chancellor, expressed himself on the important subject of the employment of Indian graduates, as follows: [1]

"Year by year a large number of young men pass out through the University to take their places among the general body of citizens, equipped with an amount of learning far beyond that which their forefathers enjoyed. It has been said that the number of highly educated youths is far ahead of the requirements of the country, and that the result

[1] Report on Public Instruction in the Madras Presidency for 1896–7, p. 55.

of the present policy is to produce a body of dissatisfied persons, unable to find a suitable opening in life, and that higher education is advancing faster than is compatible with the general progress of the people.

"It is interesting, in connection with this subject, to note that there are at the disposal of Government (Madras) 6,500 posts, carrying a monthly salary of Rs. 30 and upwards, and the annual number of vacancies amongst these posts is, approximately, 290. The yearly average number of graduates in Arts is 236, calculated on the figures of the last ten years. From this it will be seen that suitable employment is available in the Government service for a very large number of graduates, if not for all, and the figures go very far towards disproving the idea that the yearly outturn of graduates is in excess of the demand. As a matter of fact, not more than one-third of the total number of graduates whose names appear on the books of the University, have obtained appointments under Government, although, in almost all offices, preference is given to applicants who have graduated, and for some posts a University degree is held to be a necessary qualification."

Present System of Education Immature.

A writer in a representative Indian magazine [1] has pertinently reminded us of the fact that the culture of English-speaking Hindus, such as it is, is culture in its adolescence. Its faults are obvious and irritating, but they are faults inevitable to that stage. Fifty years is a very short time in the history of a nation, and it is less than fifty years since this movement in the direction of Western learning fairly got under weigh. This is hardly a long enough time in which to convert large numbers to a new culture, and exhibit in them its ripe and lovely fruits. If, hitherto, Western culture has produced some smatterers in India rather than all scholars, and mere officials rather than

[1] *The Harvest Field*, May, 1899.

men, the fault is not in the system only, but even more in the fact that it is young, and that it has important influences working counter to it. The fault of the culture of New India is not rottenness, but immaturity. "It is hard, sour, and sometimes repellent fruit, perhaps, but it has this supreme advantage over rotten fruit, that there is hope in it."

True Parallel to Roman Noble and Chinese Literati.

The parallelism with the Roman Noble and Chinese Mandarin may be more truly found in those Brahmans of India whose culture is that only of the Sanskrit and the Vernaculars. That is culture in its decadence. It has no eyes for history, and science makes no appeal to it. It has ceased to be progressive and assimilative. It makes no attempt to adapt itself to present-day movements. It abates not one jot of its old haughty claims, even though changed conditions have robbed it of its power to enforce them. It has ceased to alter character, or to enlarge ability, or to provoke originality. It survives in dignity, but with diminishing influence, for it commands none of the forces which the new times require. That is the true parallel to the vanished culture of Rome, and the vanishing culture of China.

European and Oriental Learning.

This brings us to the question of European knowledge and of the English language as the material and medium of instruction. We have outlived the arguments of the Anglicists and the Orientalists in the discussion that so largely characterized the second period of British Education in India. In more recent years this discussion seems to have revived; and the wisdom of attaching so much importance to the study of English literature, and so little to Oriental classical and vernacular literature, has again been called in question. It has been felt by some that Macaulay's influence made the pendulum swing too far in the direction of English learning, and that it would have been better if the study of Sanskrit and Arabic literature had been allowed to go hand in hand with the study of the literature of the West. In this way the breach between the past and the present might have been less perceptible, and the new knowledge might have had less unsettling effects. But however that may be, however necessary it may be to bestow greater attention in the future on the classical languages of India, there is now no forsaking of the past possible, so far as Western learning is concerned. Distinct and well-sustained efforts have been made to restore Oriental learning to a higher place in India, but in vain. The Punjab University has been largely concerned with this effort. But the Oriental Faculty attached to that University continues to be a failure, and is only saved from utter collapse by an extravagant system of scholarships. No less than two-thirds of those who can be induced to attend this Oriental College, receive scholarships and stipends. In 1898 the expenditure on this college amounted to Rs. 31,336, of which only Rs. 263 stood for the fees collected within this same period. During the ten years 1887–97 the total number of Oriental degrees was only 35. These facts justify the remark of the Chancellor of that University that "it would not be surprising if the general classes of the Oriental College were, in the course of a few years, to die of pure atrophy."

Separate Oriental Faculties in the University.

Warned by this example, it has been recently announced[1] that the committee appointed by the Senate of the Madras University to consider and report upon the proposal made by the Honourable D. Duncan, Director of Public Instruction of the Madras Presidency, to institute an Oriental side to the University, has come to the conclusion that the time has not arrived for the creation of a separate Oriental Faculty. It is also announced that that the Educational Department will now bring forward a scheme for the encouragement of Oriental

[1] *The Educational Review of India*, June, 1899.

studies and literature, by the institution of public tests in the principal classical and vernacular languages of the Presidency. The objects to be gained by this proposal are said to be: (1) The supply of competent persons for employment as teachers of Oriental languages in schools and colleges; and (2) the production of works, in the vernacular languages, especially adapted to bring within the reach of the masses of the population, useful knowledge, and to the development of the material resources of the country.

The Employment of English. We are now on the threshold of a large and practical question, the determination of the position which the English language should hold in India. Shall it take the place of the classical or the vernacular languages of the country? Dr. Miller holds that what has been done for Europe by training in the classical tongues is to be done for India by training in the English language, which, whether for better or worse, is practically the classical tongue of the Indian Universities, and of education in that land.[1]

In 1835–6, of 3,573 scholars in government schools, 1,818 were studying English. Fifty years later, English was taught, in Colleges, to over 6,000, in High schools to 60,000, and in middle schools to 75,000 students, while even in Primary schools it was studied by over 60,000 children. Thus English was being studied by 200,000 students. In the year 1896–7, this number had been more than doubled, 433,606 students being now engaged in learning English in Public institutions.

In High schools and Colleges, English is not only the subject, it is also the medium of instruction. Some of the most important newspapers which are circulated only for native readers, are printed by preference in English, and of the total number of books published each year, about one in ten is written in English. The language of national assemblies

[1] *Ibid.*, March, 1899.

in India is English, as the one common to the greatest number. Where is this increase to stop? Will it continue until English has supplanted all of the 150 troublesome vernaculars? We have mentioned the fact that Mr. Hodgson, the eminent Orientalist, championed the native dialects, and that Mr. Adam, whose reports upon indigenous education have been referred to, expressed his deep conviction of the impossibility of English ever becoming a general medium of instruction. To Mr. R. T. Thornton, however, belongs the distinction of having first advocated the *extinction* of the native languages. He argued from a parallelism between the Roman Empire and the British dominion in India. The Romans encouraged the study of Latin in Gaul, Spain and Africa. They did not promote a Gallic, Iberian or Moorish literature in their conquered provinces. Why, then, he asks, should the English encourage the native languages of India? In reply, it is only necessary to point out that the analogy of the two cases fails in the fact that the Gauls and Spaniards and Moors were not characteristically literary nations. Nor did they possess a copious literature. Nor had they for 2500 years possessed a scientific theory of grammar, and a clear analysis of the forms and structure of their languages. Had Mr. Thornton carried his analogy a little further, and endeavored to apply it to the one subject people of Rome most nearly akin to the Hindus in intellectual subtlety and moral depth, the Greeks, he would have seen its utter failure. The Greeks never gave up for Latin the language which embodied all that remained to solace them in their degradation, the memory of the ancient glories of their race, and the creations of their genius. What was true of the past is also true of more modern Grecian history. Only a century ago Greece was liberated from a Turkish tyranny centuries old, during which time her language had lost much

English and the Indian Vernaculars.

The Analogy of Greece and India.

of its strength and beauty. The modern Greeks do not speak the same language as did Pericles; they speak a language which has been, by a gradual development, derived from the classic Greek. Still they did not yield it, shorn of its glory though it was, to the language of their Moslem conquerors. Ancient classic Greek may be likened to the classical languages of the Hindus, and the modern language of Athens to the ruling vernaculars of India, which, though not Sanskrit, are some of them derived from it. Our analogy between the languages of Greece and India holds good in fact. While English is being studied by a little over 11 per cent. of the pupils in public institutions, and the classical languages, Sanskrit, Arabic and Persian, by about 8 per cent., the Vernaculars are being studied by no less than 97 per cent. In one year, of about 5,000 books issued from the presses of India, 550 were written in English, 725 in classical languages, and over 3,000 in the vernaculars. It thus appears that there is little likelihood of English supplanting the classics as the literary language of India, or of its becoming the every-day speech of the millions, who often live and die without even having heard the language of their rulers. Aside from the fact of numbers, there are many circumstances which augment this probability. The natural objects, the trees, the animals, the implements, the social order, are too different to admit of easy transition from one language to another. On every ground, it seems scarcely possible that English should ever be anything more in India than was Greek in ancient Rome.

The Influence and place of Indian Vernaculars.

Moral and Religious Instruction.

There is still another, and a far more serious problem, which we must recognize, and the discussion of which we enter upon with hesitancy, because of the delicacy of treatment required. The place of moral and religious instruction in a State system of education has always been a question of deep concern and of difficult solution. It has led also to the adoption of widely differing policies.

Ancient and Mediæval Systems. In Greece and Rome religion became a function of the State, and closely allied with their educational systems. In the Middle Ages the Church and State coalesced and formed so intimate a union that the domain of each was entered by the other. During nearly 1500 years, the religious influence was above every other. Religion taught the other branches of civilization to speak its language. Philosophy, science, art and politics were all permeated with religious theology. Their motives became religious. But, finally, a differentiation took place, and men began to distinguish between the things of Caesar and the things of God. The School, which throughout the Middle Ages, was the creation of the Church, has, in most countries, passed into the control of the Civil Government, and there has been a consequent declension in the emphasis placed upon the religious element in education.

Modern System. The attitude of the present day towards religious instruction is very divided. In Germany and France we see the working of two diametrically opposed policies. In the former religious instruction is as definitely prescribed by law as in the latter it is excluded. This may not be so surprising, as these nations represent two different races, which have always been, more or less, in antagonism. But it is not so with Great Britain and the United States, who are people of the same race. And, yet here, again, we see wide differences of policy. For, in England, education has always been largely carried on under religious auspices, and, at the present time, the controversy over the participation of the Church in education is a dominant political issue. In the United States, on the contrary, there is a complete separation of the Church and State, and the practical exclusion of definite religious instruction.

The Indian System. We may say, in general, that the secondary aim of education in Europe has been to produce gentlemen and Christians. In India religion has, for twenty-five centuries, sanctified the pursuit of knowledge, as the path to liberation from the world, and absorption in God. When the English undertook the education of India, the folly of Government interference with the religion of the Hindus was generally conceded, and they bound themselves, by repeated pledges, to the maintenance of religious neutrality. This principle, asserted by all the great Governors of India, solemnly proclaimed in the great Despatch of 1854, and reiterated in the Recommendations of the Education Commission of 1882,[1] was regarded by the Hindus as the great safeguard of their liberties. But the principle cut both ways. Stripped of all secondary and ulterior aims, Government education was confined to the primary object of conveying knowledge.

The place of Moral Training. If, as Herbert Spencer asserts, education is training for completeness of life, one of its primary elements is religion. A complete man is not one whose mind alone is active, but he is a complete man who is alive in all his faculties. And who will deny to man, and to the Hindus above many others, the possession of the religious faculty? If an educational system be established on a basis which excludes this religious element, the result will, inevitably, be a deterioration of the highest national type, and the loss of the finer qualities which are the safeguards of purity and unselfish conduct. Both physical and intellectual education are, in a large measure, practical; but, in the third element of education, the will training, we enter upon the social development of man. The natural starting point of social culture is the family, but morality is its true essence. The chief principles of morality are duty, virtue and the exercise of conscience, and education must lay stress on

[1] Resolution 25.

the truth that nothing has so much value as will guided by the right, or by the sense of duty. The actualizing of duty is virtue, and the result of the practice of virtue is the development of character. The education which trains the mind is eminently desirable, but that which forms the character is indispensable. The essential element in human life is conduct, and conduct springs from what we believe quite as much as, if not more than, from what we know.

Conduct and Character.

The Weakness of the Indian System.

And right here, what we believe to be an entirely sound educational theory has its application to the system adopted in India. The elevation of the Hindu character is admitted by intelligent Hindus, no less than by Englishmen, to be a prime necessity. The failure of the educational system to do this, to instill in them our commanding sense of duty, to lead them to a practical adoption of the virtues of morality, in a word, to give them such moral strength as is possessed by the nations of Europe after long centuries of religious instruction, this failure gives countenance to *The Spectator's* characterization of the culture of English-speaking Hindus. The religion of the Hindus is, for the educated, a philosophy, and for the ignorant, a system of observances, admitting in both cases, it is true, the conception of devotion to a God. But it has no definite scheme of morals and no religious books in which the moral element holds the highest place. Thus custom, and especially the customs of caste, were practically the sole support and authority for the morality of Brahmanism.

Western Learning and Ancient Standards.

Along with the dissolution of many ancient customs which English rule and western learning brought about, the customary morality received a grievous shock. To learn that the world was not made exclusively for the Brahmans, that the earth was not made of concentric rings, with India at the centre, and that it does not rest on the back of a tortoise, could not but have the result of shaking belief in many other vain theories of the world and of life. Elementary science taught that, whatever might be the power of the Brahman, he could not make water boil at any other temperature than that at which it naturally boils, and that a million repetitions of the names of their gods will not create a good crop without cultivation, or keep epidemics away from unsanitary homes. This decay of old influences led, among the classes affected by contact with the English, to a certain weakening of the moral sense, such as it was. The present condition of the hundreds of millions of her Indian subjects, alien in race and in religion, in sympathies and in aspirations, imposes a responsibility upon England, the magnitude of which it is almost impossible to appreciate. A Hindu gentleman of keen intelligence, recently returned from a trip to England during the Jubilee celebrations in London, said that the thought that impressed him most was the moral responsibility of England toward her Colonies and Dependencies. Intellectual progress has outstripped moral progress in India, and the bonds of ancient tradition and of religious sanction have been abruptly snapped. A generation is growing up in India of young men who have no deep religious convictions, no fixed moral principles, no well-defined ideals of conduct, "no landmark on earth, and no lode-star in heaven." The ancient Hindu ideals exist no longer, if ever, as a moral dynamic in ordinary life. "It is philosophy, not food."

Necessity for Religious Instruction.

A keenly intelligent and observing Englishman, who has lived many years in India, and moved freely among the educated classes, has recently sent out this solemn warning: "Our Indian education is creating an immense class for whom it has largely loosened the authority and obligation of the past, and who, with quickened intellectual capacities, crave for a career which we cannot afford to open, for lack of that moral fibre with which we have failed to supply them, in the place of what they have lost. Such a situation is charged with peril; and it cannot possibly stop there. We must go on to furnish those moral and spiritual forces which alone can supplement and justify the education. Our statesmen have reached the limit of their powers, and a stupendous task confronts us."[1]

Missionary Education. This need is met, in part, by the large number of schools and colleges supported by missionary societies, which form, as we have seen, so important a part of the educational system of India, and wherein religious instruction is an essential feature of the daily curriculum. That this demand for moral training exists, and that the opportunity for it is appreciated, is attested by the fact that these missionary institutions are so largely attended by non-Christian Hindus, notwithstanding, and possibly, in part, because of the definite daily instruction in the Christian religion, with the Bible as text-book; and this when ample opportunity is afforded for attending schools under Government and Hindu auspices, where no religious instruction is given.

State Institutions. But these are Private institutions receiving aid from Government. So far as Public institutions are concerned, perhaps the most advanced position taken, in regard to this important element in education, by the most thoughtful administrators in India, may be summed up in the words of the Chancellor of the Allahabad University, whose address has been frequently referred to:

"I agree with those who think that education should, from the beginning, be combined with religious teaching; but the difficulty is to effect that combination in India. The Government must observe an attitude of strict neutrality in

[1] Rev. T. E. Slater, Paper prepared for the Centenary of the L. M. S., 1895.

all religious matters, and it would be impossible for its educational officers to impart religious instruction in its schools and colleges. The only satisfactory solution to the problem, in my opinion, lies in the extension of the principle of grants-in-aid, the establishment, by independent managers and associations, of schools and colleges in which religious instruction can be freely given hand in hand with secular education. The State, looking only to the quality of secular instruction, should assist such of them as ask for assistance, either by contributions of money, or by some other suitable kind of recognition. This system seems to me to afford the only solution of the problem of how religion can be united with secular education in this country."[1]

Other questions under discussion in India.

There are many other questions of great importance to the developing educational life of India, and which are discussed with deep interest in that country. We can only mention them here.

Reforms in University Education.

Reforms in University education, with special reference to examinations, are being very warmly and generally agitated. The establishment of an "Imperial Institute," looking to the provision of a teaching staff, and a large University plant, with a distinct view to original research, has been recently made possible by the munificent endowment of a wealthy and intelligent Indian gentleman.

Technical and Industrial Education.

The development of technical and industrial education is pressed by many in authority, who see in it a means to the utilization of the large mineral and agricultural resources of the country, and to a removal of much of the poverty which so cripples the people.

Primary Education for non-caste Classes.

The wider diffusion of knowledge, and the spreading of the beneficent results that flow from it, among the masses of the lower, or

[1] *The Educational Review of India*, April, 1899.

Panchamma, classes, who compose one-sixth of the population, and who are entirely without the great caste divisions of the country, is an extension of the educational system especially urged by the missionaries in Southern India, and supported by many in authority in the Government. The Honourable Mr. D. Duncan, D. SC., LL. D., the Director of Public Instruction of the Madras Presidency, is bringing his long and distinguished career in India to a conclusion by a very judicious leadership in the development of this most important movement.

Female Education. Female education is being agitated among the Hindus, and pressed both by missionaries and the Departments of Education alike, in order to the enlargement of the social and intellectual life, now so limited by the restrictions placed upon the women of that country. The Inspectresses of Girls' Schools, by their untiring and wisely directed efforts, have done much for this cause.

Conclusion. Long as it may have seemed in the telling, the history of British education in India is not without its interest. The reaction of the West on the East and the revival of peoples everywhere visible in Japan, in India, and even in China, is a phenomenon as remarkable as any in history. In India, where a social order has been based for 2000 years on a deep philosophy, the study of this revival cannot be without attraction for those who are observing the tendencies of the time. A primitive society has suddenly awakened to find itself face to face with an enemy it is powerless to resist. The modern world, where it does not absorb, destroys. In the East, British Education is an agent at once destructive and constructive. But, whatever may be the future of the English connection with India, it is, at any rate, certain, to use again the words of the great Reformer Wilberforce, that " by planting her language, her knowledge, and her opinions in her Asiatic territories, she has put a great work beyond the reach of contingencies."

The ideas which have been introduced cannot be ineffective among a people so interested in intellectual questions as are the Hindus. They cannot but germinate, and finally change the whole face of Indian society. The present is strong and practical. The future must share many of its characteristics.

BIBLIOGRAPHY.

1. Adam, W. Report to Government of India on Education in India.
2. Chamberlain. Things Japanese. Buddhistic Education. Pp. 71, 123.
3. Chicago International Congress of Education, 1893. P. 890.
4. Copleston. Buddhism in Ceylon. Ch. 1, 3, 18, 29, 31.
5. Great Britain. Parliamentary Blue Books, East India Affairs. Reports 1812, '32–'52.
6. De Valbezen. The English and India.
7. Hopkins. The Religions of India.
8. Hunter. A Study in Indian Administration.
9. Hunter. Brief History of the Indian People. Ch. v.
10. Hunter. Imperial Gazetteer of India. Vol. vi., ch. 1, 3, 4, 16.
11. India. Progress of Education. Quinquennial Reports, 1887–92 and 1892–97.
12. India. Report of Education Commission, 1882.
13. India. Moral and Material Progress of the People of India.
14. Johnston. General Council on Education in India.
15. Johnston. Our Educational Policy in India.
16. Lanman. A Sanskrit Reader. Notes p. 295.
17. Laurie. Pre-Christian Education.
18. Lethbridge. High Education in India.
19. Madras. Educational Rules.
20. Madras. Grant-in-Aid Code.
21. Madras. Progress of Education. Quinquennial Report, 1892–97.
22. Monier-Williams. Indian Wisdom.
23. Satthianadhan. History of Education in the Madras Presidency.
24. Thomas. British Education in India.
25. Trevelyan. Education in India.
26. Whitney. A Sanskrit Grammar. Introduction.

PERIODICALS.

1. *Dublin Review.* October, 1896. An Experiment in Education.
2. *Journal of Statistical Society.* June, 1894. Condition and Prospects of Popular Education in India.
3. *Journal of Statistical Society.* June, 1883. Education in India and the Indian Commission.
4. *Missionary Review.* December, 1898. The Educated Classes of India.

VITA

THE writer was born in 1862 in Madras, India. He prepared for college at the Academy, Newburgh, N. Y. In 1882 he received the degree of B. A. from Rutgers College. In 1886 he graduated from the Theological Seminary at New Brunswick, N. J. In the same year he received the degree of M. A. from Rutgers College.

After some years' residence in India, during which he engaged in educational and other work, he returned to America, and completing a course of study in Church History under the direction of the Faculty of the Divinity School mentioned above, he received the degree of B. D. from Rutgers College in 1899. He pursued studies in Education and Philosophy in Columbia University during the years 1898–1899.